OTHER BOOKS CO-AUTHORED BY FRANK BONKOWSKI

English as a Second Language

Take Series: Take One, Take Two, Take Action, Take a Look, and *Take Over*
Tapestry: Thresholds in Reading
Canadian Snapshots: Vol. 1 *Linking to the community,* Vol. 2 *Raising Issues*
Right On! Adventure in English Series

Books Just for Fun

50 Ways to Increase Your Happiness

Frank Bonkowski, Ph.D.
with Craig Gonzales

Frank Bonkowski and Craig Gonzales have written a marvelous book for non-native English speakers who have advanced reading and oral comprehension skills and now want attain an equivalent level in business writing. They focus on the thought process that goes into effective writing rather making the reader work through a series of writing drills. They explain their points using the techniques espoused in the book: plain, simple English with easy-to-understand examples. By also providing language-learning techniques, the authors give readers tools to continue increasing their vocabulary long after they have finished reading the book. Write Now is the thinking man's conduit to effective English business writing.

Steven Bleau
Instructional Designer,
FGL Sports

Write Now: Business Writing that Gets Results is a clear, thorough resource for anyone that needs to learn professional writing, or brush up on potentially rusty skills. The book is well laid out, logical in progression, and includes activities and practice exercises that are surprisingly challenging - even to those of us who make a living writing in English! If you were going to pick one professional writing book to get you through your career, it should be this one. From the goals of writing, from identifying your reader to accounting for jargon - Craig and Frank have got you covered.

Danny Iny
Firepole Marketing

Very well-organized and comprehensive! Definitely different from everything else I've seen out there in the sense that it has a first-person account of how to effectively tackle the writing process. Write Now is a great tool for all levels!

Maia Williamson
Language Instructor,
Royal Military College

Really great stuff. Easy to understand, logical and valuable. This will be a book that I will keep handy as a reference tool and guide. I must see 10 resumes per week and I would estimate about eight out of ten are problematic. Poor grammar, typos, run on sentences, and weak structure. This leads me to think that there are many people who could benefit from this book. I would gladly recommend Write Now and will begin by encouraging my four daughters to pick up a copy of it.

Mark Yerbury
President
Qualiteam Inc
A Dale Carnegie Franchise

 CONTENTS

2. PLAN PROPERLY   31

3. STRUCTURE THE DOCUMENT   57

5. KNOW HOW TO SELF-EDIT 97

ACKNOWLEDGEMENTS

This book would not have been possible without the unwavering support, encouragement, and creative input of my family, business partner, colleagues, design team, and editor.

Jacqueline, my wife, soul mate, and e-lady, is always present and ever willing to share imaginative ideas in any of my business projects. Why e-lady? She brings excitement and electricity to my life. Thanks also go to my two step-daughters, Valérie and Andrea, for their love, first of all, and their valuable comments on the style and look of the book.

Many thanks go to Craig Gonzales, my business partner, for his youthful energy, insightful comments, and technical wizardry. He keeps pushing me to find new ways of providing value to readers. In a stroke of inspiration, he came up with the title and subtitle to the book.

I want to thank Toni LaMotta, my midlife mentor (www.tonilamotta.com), for introducing me to the wide world of CreateSpace and Kindle. In our weekly conversations, she always amazes me with her clever ideas and ingenious thinking about writing and publishing as well as being of service to others.

A word of thanks goes to Fred Horowitz (http://fredhorowitz.com/), my former business coach. He continues to be a source of inspiration and enlightenment about living the created life.

Kudos go to the book design team at Office Systems Technology: Micropublishing and Hypermedia, Vanier College, Montreal (http://www.vaniercollege.qc.ca/micromedia). It was such a pleasure to work with Joan Taylor, department head, and Shari Blaukopf, lead teacher on the project. They put together a remarkable design team made up of Cassandra Carosello, Chelsia Bissonnette, Precilla Daria, Heidi De Paoli, Felicia Vendette and Tharsiny Thuraichamy.

Thanks to our editor, Kristina Brune (www.uppercaseediting.com), for fine-tuning the book and putting it in top shape.

I am so grateful for all this support. Again, thanks to you all for being there.

■ INTRODUCTION

Why You Need This Book

English is today's language of global communication and international business. It is estimated that globally up to one billion people speak some form of English. Writing English correctly is vitally important to your business success.

There are three times as many non-native English ("non-NE") speakers as native speakers in the world. In addition, there exist many varieties of English across countries and cultures. While English accents, idioms, and turns-of-phrase may change from country to country, professional English writing is stable the world over – if you write well, you gain respect and improve your professional life.

So what can a high level of written English do for you? If you are beginning your professional career, you could use effective business writing to move ahead faster. You may need English to write a **CV**, a job application, a letter, a **start-up** proposal, or a business plan.

On the other hand, you may be an **experienced** freelance consultant, a manager, or owner of a company. You need high-level business writing skills to gain a competitive **edge**. Through informative and persuasive writing, you could better hold your reader's attention, sell your products or services, or motivate your employees.

When you are speaking or giving a presentation, you can rely to a great extent on your body language and voice to get your message across. In writing, however, you don't have those tools to count on. You have to use the power of your words to convey your message. In addition, as a non-NE speaker you have another **challenge** in expressing yourself effectively in writing: *English is not your first language.*

To counter that fact, I recommend that you take a systematic approach to writing:

* Be clear about what you want to say and who your audience is.

* Plan your writing so you know what you are writing about and the message you want to communicate.

* Develop a writing plan.

* Review the message and the language to see if readers will correctly interpret your writing.

If you can do these things effectively, readers will respond positively to your message. Our book gives you plenty of necessary information that will help you greatly improve your business writing. But it is up to you to ensure the writing is error-free and effective - information without review is pointless.

Language-learning activities

Throughout this book we will give you many different kinds of language-learning activities that will build your vocabulary, comprehension, and writing skills.

A strong vocabulary is essential for strong writing. While you don't need a professor's level of vocabulary, words do convey meaning. Knowing more words will help you be more precise in your writing. These activities – matching words and their meaning, writing completing sentences, writing definitions of words – will teach you some very common business writing vocabulary.

There are also many reading comprehension questions – true and false, matching, and

INTRODUCTION

question and answer – to sharpen your reading skills. Writing activities will help you practice revising a text and vary the kinds of sentences you use.

Please work through these activities before checking the suggested answers in the answer
key. Be sure to apply what you learn.

◼ OVERVIEW OF THE WRITING PROCESS

Throughout my career I've written many business documents as a freelance consultant and entrepreneur. I've also taught academic writing as a college teacher.

This experience has allowed me to simplify the **fundamentals** of business writing into 15 key **elements** - divided into five categories - in this guide to business writing.

1. UNDERSTAND YOUR FOCUS

For business writing to be effective and persuasive, you have to be aware of the goals of your writing and the context in which your writing will be received.

Therefore, you need to:

Step 1. Know Your Purpose – why are you writing?

Step 2. Picture Your Audience – who are you writing to?

Step 3. Understand the Situation – what is the context in which you are writing?

2. PLAN PROPERLY

Lewis Carroll, author of *Alice in Wonderland*, once said, "If you don't know where you are going, any road will take you there." Another of my favorite quotes is: "He who fails to plan, plans to fail." These are not good practices if you want to succeed in business.

In order to put yourself on the road to success, you must be able to:

Step 4. Brainstorm Ideas – how do you come up with ideas and how do you organize them?

Step 5. Research the Facts – how do you know what you are looking for and how do you find it?

Step 6. Ask questions – what are the tools for getting the right people to provide you information, **insights**, or testimonials?

3. STRUCTURE YOUR DOCUMENT

Many tips and strategies for organizing a presentation or speaking engagement, such as developing an outline and sequencing your ideas in logical ways, can apply to structuring writing too, especially in formal documents such as a report.

You need to know how to:

Step 7. Make an Outline – how do you lay out ideas in a logical and orderly way to help the reader follow a message?

Step 8. Write a Draft – how do you begin the writing process and construct coherent paragraphs?

Step 9. Develop the Message – how do you make your arguments clear to the reader?

4. USE APPROPRIATE WRITING STYLE

Business writing is very different from academic writing or literary writing – I know since I have taught both for many years. Business writing is about being simple, **succinct**, and clear in your message to inform or persuade the reader. It does not always have to be complex and formal or involve artistic expression.

For this reason, you need to work on these three elements:

Step 10. Practice Clear Writing – how can you be concise and direct in your writing?

Step 11. Project the Right Tone – how do you show the right attitude to the reader?

Step 12. Develop Your Style – how do you create an effective business writing voice?

5. KNOW HOW TO SELF-EDIT

As a business professional, it is absolutely critical to get your message right, especially when the **stakes** are high. You would never think of attending a business meeting with your hair uncombed or your face unshaven. So why would you send a business document that is still a **draft**?

You must be able to:

Step 13. Revise the Contents – how do you write a crystal clear document that accomplishes its objective?

Step 14. Edit the Language– how do you improve the choice of words and sentences?

Step 15. Proofread for Perfection – how do you check the document for mechanical errors in grammar, spelling, and punctuation?

ACTIVITIES

ACTIVITY 1. WORD POWER

Having a strong vocabulary is essential for doing well professionally. In this exercise, we ask you to figure out the meaning of many words in **bold** we referred to in the text. If you know them all, that is great. If you do not, then we hope you learn them now.

Match the word or expression from the article on the left with its correct meaning on the right.

Word or expression	Meaning	Choices
1. CV	_____	a. deep understanding
2. Jot down	_____	b. advantage
3. Lay out	_____	c. test of your ability
4. Succinct	_____	d. a business just starting
5. Draft	_____	e. basics
6. Edge	_____	f. arrangement
7. Insight	_____	g. distinctive style
8. Fundamentals	_____	h. stage of a plan
9. Start-up	_____	i. component
10. Elements	_____	j. write
11. Stake	_____	k. résumé
12. Voice	_____	l. concise
13. Challenge	_____	m. share or interest

WRITE NOW: BUSINESS WRITING THAT GETS RESULTS

ACTIVITIES

ACTIVITY 2. READ TO UNDERSTAND

Mark each statement as T (true) or F (false) according to information in the text.

Statement	T / F
1. A written business document usually goes through several drafts.	_____
2. The most important document you will ever write is a business plan.	_____
3. One of the main goals of business writing is to give your opinion on a topic.	_____
4. What is essential in planning is getting your facts correct.	_____
5. A good way to improve your writing is to review your document with a critical eye.	_____
6. Never assume that your audience has all the information necessary to understand your message.	_____
7. In business writing an effective style is based on creativity and imagination.	_____
8. There is really only one standard way to write in English.	_____

ANSWERS TO ACTIVITIES ■

ANSWERS • **ACTIVITY 1. WORD POWER**

Word or expression	Meaning	Choices
1. CV	k	a. deep understanding
2. Jot down	j	b. advantage
3. Lay out	f	c. test of your ability
4. Succinct	l	d. a business just starting
5. Draft	h	e. basics
6. Edge	b	f. arrangement
7. Insight	a	g. distinctive style
8. Fundamentals	e	h. stage of a plan
9. Start-up	d	i. component
10. Elements	i	j. write
11. Stake	m	k. résumé
12. Voice	g	l. concise
13. Challenge	c	m. share or interest

ANSWERS TO ACTIVITIES

ANSWERS • ACTIVITY 2. READ TO UNDERSTAND

Statement	T / F
1. A written business document usually goes through several drafts.	T
2. The most important document you will ever write is a business plan.	F
3. One of the main goals of business writing is to give your opinion on a topic.	F
4. What is essential in planning is getting your facts correct.	T
5. A good way to improve your writing is to review your document with a critical eye.	T
6. Never assume that your audience has all the information necessary to understand your message.	T
7. In business writing an effective style is based on creativity and imagination.	F
8. There is really only one standard way to write in English.	F

UNDERSTAND YOUR FOCUS

1. UNDERSTAND YOUR FOCUS

It is critically important to write English correctly when you hope to advance your career or your business prospects. This is true for several reasons.

First, you want to provide proof that you are educated and know what you are talking about. In film and television, one of the quickest ways that wealth is indicated is to attach painstakingly accurate grammar and pronunciation to the characters. Just as in social situations, proof of competency in business is often determined within the first few moments of talking with someone. The quickest way to lose the respect of the people you are working with is to write incorrect English; it just looks bad.

Second, you need to express yourself clearly the first time you write. The purpose of writing is to convey your message. You don't want colleagues and clients to have to guess your meaning or become distracted by mistakes. You will also impress others who are struggling with their own English — you will be seen as the expert.

Finally, you want to be able to build relationships with people throughout your organization and the world. Multilingual people are able to communicate with more people than those who are only unilingual. English is the language of record, so speaking and writing English well opens your network to people of import throughout the world.

Before you start writing, however, you are going to have to plan, pre-plan, and focus on your writing. You cannot just write what you feel; you must plan your writing. This is essential for those trying to express themselves — words don't just magically come out of our fingers; everything we do should be planned in advance with your goals in mind.

Before you do anything in life, you must set goals. Without goals, you would wander aimlessly along. Some goals are simple: *get food*. Other goals are more difficult: *make one million dollars*. But all action you take — be it in writing or in work — should be towards a specific and actionable goal. In business both you and your clients have a goal in mind. Those goals directly affect your writing.

You should always have a clear idea of the **goals** of your writing and the situations you are in. You should always focus your message on your audience. You have to understand your readers and their goals. Always consider the reader's point of view for any type of business document you write.

STEP 1. Know Your Purpose

Make your work to be in keeping with your purpose.
Leonardo da Vinci

Da Vinci speaks the truth, and you can take his lesson to mean many things. For your writing, you must always create towards the end goal. Every word of this book is crafted to lead you to several conclusions. The purpose of this chapter, for example, is to convince you that you need a purpose for your writing: **you need a goal.**

It is critical to know the main message, purpose, and goal of your document. Consequently, you have to be clear about what you want to achieve.

According to Mary Ellen Guffey, author of *Business Communication: Process and Product*, business writing can have three main purposes: **to inform, to persuade,** or **to build good will.** Let's look at the first two points.

INFORM YOUR READER

Informing your reader means to give information, instructions, or ideas. You want the person to gain information. Whenever you write a weekly report for your boss, you are informing him or her. Whenever you tell your staff how to do something, you are informing them.

If you want to inform your audience, you will be doing some of the following:

- describing or explaining a process (e.g., The first step in the process is . . .)

- defining new terms or procedures (e.g., The purpose of the new system is . . .)

- reviewing new or existing policies (e.g., Let's let look over what I've been talking about.)

- making an announcement (e.g., As a result of the latest findings, we have decided to . . .)

- giving instructions (e.g., May I recommend . . .?)

- **advising** staff or upper management about new developments (e.g., We recently learned that . . .)

- demonstrating how something works (e.g., Perhaps I could start off by saying that ...)

- illustrating different sides of an argument (e.g., I see your point, but . . .)

- **synthesizing** information from different sources (e.g., So, to sum up . . .)

- answering questions or enquiries. (e.g., I'm glad you asked that question.)

PERSUADE YOUR READER

Persuasion is the art of convincing people to believe what you want them to believe and do what you want them to do. It happens every day, in both our professional and personal lives. Whenever you ask for a raise, you are trying to persuade your boss to believe that you are worth more money. Whenever you try to make a sale, you are trying to persuade a prospect that you have the product or service she desires.

If your purpose is to persuade your readers, you could:

- convince others of your point of view (e.g., If you allow me to make a suggestion, why don't you . . .?)

* influence the thinking of your colleague or superiors (e.g., I would like to suggest that . . .)

* argue a point of view (e.g., That sounds interesting, but I would prefer to . . .)

* recommend a plan of action (e.g., Our advice is to . . .)

* change existing thinking (e.g., Have you thought about . . . ?)

* **advocate** different options (e.g., That may be true. However, we recommend you consider . . .)

* **urge** your readers to take action (e.g., Please let us know your decision as soon as possible.)

* defend a unpopular point of view (e.g., We see things differently.)

* justify a decision you made (e.g., We are absolutely sure that . . .)

* support a colleague. (e.g., We can assure you that . . .)

This lets you understand that knowing your purpose keeps you focused and ensures that your documents reflects your goal from beginning to end. It also helps you determine the most appropriate method of communication, such as a fax, email, phone call, meeting, or letter.

The key to business writing is clarity — a topic we'll explore much more in Step 10. You are a busy person, and whomever you are writing to is also a busy person. You **must** write your intention very early in your message. A common practice is to start your letter with:

> *I am writing to [ask for / tell you] _____.*

Once you state your **purpose**, you can begin either informing or persuading your reader. This shows **respect for her time** and **awareness of the complexity of business**. You must prepare your reader for what you will write about.

In addition, by doing so, you are letting yourself know how and what to write. If you want to argue a point of view, for example, you will have to write an argumentative style and provide facts to support your conclusion. However, if you are trying to recommend a plan of action, you will want to calm fears with supportive language. **The goal of your writing determines the style of your writing.**

HOW TO CREATE YOUR GOAL

This how-to should be self-evident. Whenever you sit down to write you should know *why* you are writing. For example, Craig, who tutors students, shared with me this story. A prospective student told him that she was not interested in studying with him. She decided to study with someone else. He had to respond with an email; he realized that he couldn't just let that go silently… he felt it deserved a response.

Before he wrote his response, however, he had to decide what he wanted. He could try to inform her that statistically speaking, his course was the best. Or he could try to inform her that the other course was rubbish. He could try to persuade her to reconsider, alleviating any fears she may have had, or he could try to persuade her to try both courses and pick the winner later.

Ultimately, he decided to inform her that he would be around after she finished her other course in case she needed extra help. **This goal** — to wish her the best and offer support down the road **— structured his entire email response**.

He asked himself one very simple question: *What do I want from this?*

He then wrote that down. He knew his goal, his purpose, and what he would do. From there, he had to move on to step two – *understanding who he was writing to.*

ACTION CHECKLIST FOR STEP 1

	Yes
1. I know what I want to accomplish.	
2. I want to • inform. • persuade. • build good will.	
3. I know specifically what I want to do to INFORM the reader - for example, describe or explain a process.	
4. I know specifically what I want to do to PERSUADE the reader - for example, convince others of my point of view.	
5. I will write a • fax • email • letter • report • other type of document.	

STEP 2. Picture Your Audience

Writing comes more easily if you have something to say.
Sholem Asch

While Asch speaks the truth — you know those people who say a lot without saying anything at all, versus those who use their words for maximum impact — he forgot to mention that WHO you speak to determines WHAT you say.

Imagine writing an email to your sweetheart and then imagine writing that same email to your boss! There is no way that writing those two documents with the same tone would end well. One style of writing does not fit all readers of your writing. You need to clearly picture your audience if you want to create writing that truly speaks to them. There is no way you will achieve your purpose if you don't know who you are writing to.

QUESTIONS TO ASK ABOUT YOUR READER

As you start thinking about your reader, ask yourself these questions:

- What is their **background**?

- What experience do they have?

- What is their education?

- Am I writing internally for co-workers or for management?

- Am I addressing customers or a general audience?

Knowing who your audience is will help you determine the tone and level of formality. It will also help you correct any **biases** you may have. For example, as I am a man, I may expect all my readers are male as well. Therefore, in writing a letter, I may only use the words, "Dear Sir." This, however, is very wrong. Since English grammar gives us masculine and feminine pronouns, it's best to mix and match throughout your writing or use the plural form, to stay fresh and to avoid gender bias.

Dale Fitzpatrick and Kathleen Vance, authors of *Writing for Success: Preparing for Business, Technology, Trades and Career Programs*, recommend you include all the possible readers you can think of when you write.

They also suggest that you come up with probable questions that readers may have in mind. You should answer those questions in your writing. This will help you establish a) what to say, b) the order you say it, and c) the level of detail or explanation you give.

By doing this, you put yourself in the position of the reader and it makes your writing more clear and understandable. Be clear about what the reader needs to know first. Then follow it up with any other details the reader needs to know or that support your goal.

If you are writing, for example, a personal letter for admission to a business school, you might want to complete this plan.

A PLAN FOR WRITING A PERSONAL ESSAY

Who will read the letter?	Admissions director at a graduate business school
What should I tell my reader first?	That I want to apply to the school's online executive MBA program
What other things should I tell the reader?	The reasons for which I am applying My initial work experience Experience and knowledge I acquired in other departments My most recent professional accomplishments What I hope to gain from the program

ACTION CHECKLIST FOR STEP 2

	Yes
1. I know exactly to whom I am writing.	
2. I am aware of their background, experience, education and position.	
3. I have avoided any bias in my writing by using correct pronouns.	
4. I have included just the right degree of detail and explanation.	
5. I have thought about what I want to communicate to the reader.	

STEP 3. Understand the Situation

There are three rules for writing. Unfortunately, no one can agree what they are.
Somerset Maugham

People are selfish. Don't be shocked — I am selfish and you are selfish. Knowing that, you can craft your writing to feed into the selfishness of your reader. If you want to write well — that is, if you want to inform or persuade — you must know what your readers need or want to know.

The first two steps towards this are abundantly clear: *we must know our purpose and know our reader.* The next simply involves linking those two things together — figuring out how to achieve your purpose based on different types of readers.

READER PURPOSES

Readers may engage in your writing for different purposes. Owl, the Purdue Online Writing Lab, makes an interesting distinction between the purposes of more active and more passive readers.

A more active audience will read for some of the following purposes:

* to examine

* to quantify

* to assess, evaluate, or judge

* to make better decisions

- to judge, criticize, or make fun of

- to disprove.

A more passive audience will have much different purposes for reading:

- to review

- to be reassured

- to be entertained or inspired

- to enjoy, understand, or learn

- to get instruction

- to hear advice.

Make sure you know who your readers are. This will guide you in tailoring your message to their specific needs, whether it is to evaluate or simply enjoy your writing. Developing this writing skill will make you a more effective communicator.

ACTION CHECKLIST FOR STEP 3

	Yes
1. I know that my reader is • active • passive.	
2. If my reader is more ACTIVE, I know what I wish to accomplish, for example, to help readers in their decision making.	
3. If my reader is more PASSIVE, I know what I wish to accomplish, for example, to teach readers a new concept or approach.	

WRAP-UP

You now know why you are writing, to whom you are writing, and what your readers want to know. These are the first three steps in achieving your purpose.

Now that you are familiar with your audience, you can plan your document so it fits their interests and needs.

In Step 1, Know Your Purpose, you put yourself in a position to decide what:

•   purposes you have in mind - whether it is to inform, persuade, or create good will;

•   kinds of information to include or to leave out in your document; and

•   kind of introduction that would be most compelling.

In Step 2, Picture Your Audience, you decided what:

* level of formality is most appropriate (formal, semi-formal, or informal);

* background information to provide as context;

* biases to pay attention to.

In Step 3, Understand the Situation, you learned the importance of:

* whether your reader is more active or more passive; and

* examples, illustrations, or stories that will help readers better understand your point.

In the next pre-writing phase, **Plan Properly**, we'll look at three good tools for gathering content ideas: *brainstorming, doing research, and asking questions.*

ACTIVITIES

ACTIVITY 1. WORD POWER

This activity helps you build a strong vocabulary, which is essential for doing well professionally. Try to figure out the meaning of many words in **bold** referred to in the text. If you know them all, that is so great. If not, learn them now.

Match the word or expression from the article on the left with its correct meaning on the right.

Word or expression	Meaning	Choice
1. Goal	_____	a. Show to be false
2. Purpose	_____	b. Drive forward
3. Advise	_____	c. A person's history
4. Synthesize	_____	d. Accomplish
5. Advocate	_____	e. Intention
6. Urge	_____	f. Prejudice
7. Expect	_____	g. Take for granted
8. Background	_____	h. Objective
9. Bias	_____	i. Analyze
10. Assume	_____	j. Look forward to
11. Disprove	_____	k. Recommend
12. Achieve	_____	l. Speak in favor of

ACTIVITIES

ACTIVITY 2. QUESTION AND ANSWER

Match the question and the answer.

1. What are some ways to inform your audience?

2. What do passive readers do?

3. What should you know about your audience?

4. What do active readers like to do?

5. What is a good way to persuade your audience?

6. How can you overcome your biases?

a. Think of everyone in your audience.

b. They like to form an evaluation.

c. They read the entire text.

d. You can respond to enquiries and analyze information.

e. They like to get suggestions or be motivated.

f. You should know their level of knowledge.

g. Try giving evidence in support of your view.

h. Using graphics is essential.

ANSWERS TO ACTIVITIES

ANSWERS · **ACTIVITY 1. WORD POWER**

Word or expression	Meaning	Choice
1. Goal	**h**	a. Show to be false
2. Purpose	**e**	b. Drive forward
3. Advise	**k**	c. A person's history
4. Synthesize	**i**	d. Accomplish
5. Advocate	**l**	e. Intention
6. Urge	**b**	f. Prejudice
7. Expect	**j**	g. Take for granted
8. Background	**c**	h. Objective
9. Bias	**f**	i. Analyze
10. Assume	**g**	j. Look forward to
11. Disprove	**a**	k. Recommend
12. Achieve	**d**	l. Speak in favor of

ANSWERS TO ACTIVITIES ▪

ANSWERS · ACTIVITY 2. QUESTION AND ANSWER

1. What are some ways to inform your audience? **d**

2. What do passive readers do? **e**

3. What should you know about your audience? **f**

4. What do active readers like to do? **b**

5. What is a good way to persuade your audience? **g**

6. How can you overcome your biases? **a**

a. Think of everyone in your audience.

b. They like to form an evaluation.

c. They read the entire text.

d. You can respond to enquiries and analyze information.

e. They like to get suggestions or be motivated.

f. You should know their level of knowledge.

g. Try giving evidence in support of your view.

h. Using graphics is essential.

2. PLAN PROPERLY

Before you start writing, you must plan your entire work. For example, before you begin writing a report, you need to fully understand what you are going to write. This involves outlining, finding, and gathering information.

The goal of the planning stage is ensure you have all of the information you need to construct a piece of writing that informs or persuades. You cannot inform your boss about your financial reports if you do not do the necessary research about the company's income and expenses. You cannot ask for a raise without providing excellent reasons why you deserve the raise. Likewise, you cannot except to inform or persuade your readers without educating yourself first.

Witting at your computer hoping to write a persuasive sales email without first constructing your argument, verifying your facts, and solving any potential question will be useless and lead to a waste of time. You must use every minute well.

Like many things in life, planning is 90% of the work you do. Professional athletes compete for a few hours per week, yet they prepare many times that. Musicians might perform a two-hour concert twice per week, but you had better believe they've been practicing 40 hours per week for nearly their entire lives.

If a professional plans her craft, don't you think you should be fully prepared before you sit down and try to write it? Absolutely - especially if you are a non-native English speaker. In this section we cover the three essential techniques that I often use when writing: **brainstorming**, **researching**, and **asking questions**.

STEP 4. Brainstorm Ideas

The scariest moment is always just before you start.
Stephen King

Planning your writing is a scary and creative process. Once you know who you are going to write to, what you hope to achieve, and how you are going to explain what you want to, you have to start the arduous, yet exhilarating, task of gathering enough background information to make a great case.

A WORK-RELATED BRAINSTORMING EXAMPLE

My business partner, Craig, used to work for a publishing company. When his boss' daughter was getting married, Craig wanted to write his boss a note of congratulations. The **purpose** of his writing was to build good will with his boss and persuade him into believing he was kind and honest. The **person** he was writing to was his boss, obviously, supervised him and whom he had to respect and work for.

His boss **wanted to know** that his employees were honest and thoughtful enough to respect him. Once Craig figured that out, he sat down to prepare his letter. In this case, the only research he had to do was find out the wedding date, the girl´s name, and the name of her future husband. That way he could say something specific. He got that information from the Internet registration.

So he did his **research**. When he sat down to prepare, he did something called **brainstorming**. Basically, he wrote down his purpose and then listed all the things that he might want to write about.

32   **WRITE NOW: BUSINESS WRITING THAT GETS RESULTS**

This is the result of Craig's brainstorming session:

◊   Purpose: Tell the boss congratulations so he likes me more

- Wish him well
- Talk about her hobbies
- Talk about his hobbies
- Make a joke (?)
- Offer support in any way

This is not an exercise in creating the absolute structure of his letter. Instead, it was a creative look at all the things he wanted to do in his letter. He had his purpose and his target reader in mind, and he knew who his reader was and what he wanted to hear. So Craig could then very logically create an idea about what should be included.

HOW TO BRAINSTORM

First, when brainstorming, it's important to note that location and materials are irrelevant. There are times when I brainstorm over a long walk, a job, or a swim. Other times I'll sit down on my sofa and have a "proper think."

Other times I'll be at a café with my cell phone on record and my ideas flowing. **When you start to create the "what will I write about" brainstorm, there is no hard and fast rule about where you should be and what you should be doing.**

For example, when I was preparing another book, *30 Common Writing Mistakes*, I was taking a shower and thought about all the possible areas in which non-NE speakers could make mistakes.

I actually had to streak across my house so I could quickly write my ideas on the computer before I lost them. I came up with this short list: style, grammar, vocabulary, punctuation, spelling, and capitalization. Inspiration can hit anywhere, and the art of preparing your writing is to allow your mind to think freely about what you want to write about.

Second, once you realize that location does not matter, you actually have to get into the act of brainstorming. Working through ideas to get an idea of what you want to write is more art than science, because only you know who your target audience is, what you will write about, and why you are writing.

Brainstorming involves freely working through sources of inspiration to find ideas, topics, details, and theories behind what you want to write. For example, I may refer to a good book, article, or website related to what I want to write about. When Craig was writing the letter to his boss, he thought of using Google to search "How to congratulate a boss."

Amazon books (especially the book reviews) and YouTube are great places to search for discussions. If you were writing a persuasion letter to convince your boss to give you a raise, you might type in YouTube "How to ask for a raise." I suggest you keep track of all the ideas you have as you're researching so you don't forget any key points you want to make. I take notes on what I've learned either the old-fashioned way - writing them down on paper - or typing them into a Word document or a Google Drive document.

Third, in order to gather my ideas, I use the technique of mind mapping. Mind mapping is a structure and brainstorming technique used by many people to build relationships between ideas. It is a very useful strategy for seeing relationships and getting all of your writing ideas onto paper. It is a visual way to generate structure and classify words, ideas, tasks or whatever relates to the topic.

Here is an example of a mind map:

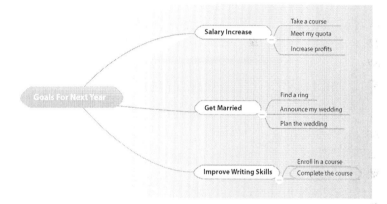

Finally, I sometimes ask myself questions about the topic. Asking myself questions during the brainstorming process can give me ideas for my list and for my mind map.

A useful tool to use is the common information-gathering technique called the 5Ws plus H.

- Who is it about?
- What happened?
- When did it occur?
- Where did it happen?
- Why did it happen?
- How did it happen?

Rudyard Kipling popularized this information-gathering approach in his **Just So Stories** (1902):

I keep six honest serving-men
(They taught me all I knew);
Their names are What and Why and When
And How and Where and Who.

Let's look at some examples of the 5Ws plus H. If you are preparing a business proposal you might want to ask yourself these questions.

QUESTIONS FOR WRITING A BUSINESS PROPOSAL

Who?	**Who** is your client? Go beyond the basic information. Know their reputation, mission statement, and corporate history.
What?	**What** does the client want from you? Be aware of the products and services your client offers. Understand the scope of the project.
Where?	**Where** is your client located? Be aware of how this will affect working conditions. Know what the primary language of the client is.

When?	**When** does the client expect the project to be delivered? Know if the client is ready to negotiate the delivery date. Agree on a date and get it in writing.
Why?	**Why** is the client doing the project? Understand the client's motivation. Be aware of other projects the client may be involved in.
How?	**How** does the client want the project done? Be aware of the kinds of tools or software the client prefers using. Understand how the client plans on using the product.

ACTION CHECKLIST FOR STEP 4

	YES
1. I know my purpose in writing - for example, to impress my boss.	
2. I write down my ideas as soon as they come to mind.	
3. I use Amazon books and YouTube to get ideas by typing in the right keywords that fit my topic.	
4. I use a mind map to lay out my ideas visually.	
5. I ask myself lots of questions about the topic using the 5Ws plus H.	

STEP 5. Research the Facts

Research is formalized curiosity. It is poking and prying with a purpose.
Zora Neale Hurston

Brainstorming helps you identify and arrange all the pieces of your writing. By the time you're ready to research, you know why you are writing, who you are writing to, what you need to say, and have an outline of what you want to talk about. But many times throughout writing you are going to need to provide facts, figures, and data. In short, you are going to have to do research.

Research is the *work* that I do. Writing is just expressing the work in a way people can understand and relate to. So when I do research I take the ideas and facts I have found and put them down on paper.

Research can be intensive, like when you do a case study or read an academic source. Or research can be informal, like checking Facebook to find out your boss' wife's name. When I say that research is essential for success in writing, I simply mean that you are going to have to use tools – *most likely the Internet* – to find the information that you don't currently have to perform your goal (inform or persuade).

My number one research tool is the Internet. There is more material on any topic than you could ever read or listen to: web pages, blogs, PDF documents, ebooks, video and audio, press releases, discussions lists and so on. You can even find academic resources if you are writing a very scholarly report for work.

The Internet is your source of knowledge – it is where you will conduct your research and find the information you need. Google.com will become your best friend, Wikipedia will help you find small facts, and Facebook will help you do cyber-research on your social network.

HOW TO USE THE INTERNET

If you are going to use the Internet for your research, here is what you should do:

◊ What is your topic? Of all the notes you made in brainstorming, which require knowledge or facts that you don't currently have?

- Go to Google and ask the question using good keywords or phrases
  - Read the pages
  - Copy and bookmark those with useful and reliable information
- Go to Wikipedia and search for the question
  - Read the page
  - Copy and bookmark those with useful and reliable information
- Go to the social networks and hunt for the information

I also use books, newspapers, scholarly journals, and magazines at the two local universities I attended: McGill and Concordia. Montreal's main city library, known as the "Bibliothèque et Archive Nationales du Québec" makes available a marvelous collection of online resources in English, such as ebooks, audio books, government and legal information, as well as newspapers.

If you cannot find what you are looking for online, go to your university library, ask a librarian for help, and hunt down printed sources of knowledge. If you are writing an email to a colleague, you won't need much library research, but if you are writing a proposal, you may very well need to use data or talk about specific topics that you may not be 100% familiar with. Then, the Internet and the library are your best friends.

Another excellent online source for business research is the Rutgers University Business Research Guide (http://libguides.rutgers.edu/business). It helps you do research on a multitude of business and management topics. It offers descriptions of databases and hundreds of reference books. There are also links to more than 3,000 selected business and management-related Internet resources.

FOUR IMPORTANT TECHNIQUES FOR REWRITING RESEARCH

Whenever you find data that you would like to put in your written work, you must put that information into your brain and into your writing in a way that is easy to understand and access. There are four techniques that you can use to ensure you retain the information and write it well.

1. Note taking. I like to use standard or legal size paper and write with abbreviations, such as "&" for and, "#" for number, and "sth" for something. There is not enough space in this book to cover proper note-taking for business writing, but please note that if you can figure out a way to outline, map, and paraphrase what you read in your research, the amount of time you take to write will significantly decrease. Note taking is the art of synthesizing information that you learn and putting it in ways that you personally understand.

2. Using direct and indirect quotes. To illustrate and support the ideas I want to develop, I use information from other sources. Quoting other sources in your written work, especially for informative writing, guarantees authority behind your information. People don't like to be informed with your opinions.

Using a credible source to quote from helps convince the reader that you mean what you say. When your boss reads a memo with a quote from a business leader, she is more likely to trust your thesis. Direct quotes use the exact words of the text being cited. Indirect quotes change the words slightly.

Direct quote:

> Frank wrote, "I also use books, newspapers, scholarly journals, and magazine at the main city library."

Indirect quote (note the change in the pronoun and the verb):

> Frank wrote that he also uses books, newspapers, scholarly journals, and magazines at the main city library.

3. Paraphrasing. Paraphrasing is the art of converting complex ideas into bullet points *(much like an MBA education)*. Paraphrasing is restating information from another text in your own words. The key to good note taking, test taking, and business writing is paraphrasing. Whenever you read, your mind naturally paraphrases what you read. This is because you don't always understand sentences on their own; rather, you have to simplify sentences to get exactly what they mean.

Here is an example:

Original Quote:

> Brainstorming involves freely working through sources of inspiration to find ideas, topics, details, and theories behind what you want to write.

Paraphrase:

> Brainstorming is technique in which you make a list of the topics and ideas you may want to write about.

4. Summarizing. Summarizing is stating the general ideas of a text in your own words. It is different from paraphrasing in that paraphrasing wants you to re-state each paragraph in simple terms.

A summary, on the other hand, just wants you to restate the main idea (not always written in the text) instead of every detail. Summaries are overviews; paraphrases help you create a mental map. This is a key skill that requires you to synthesize and rephrase the essential ideas.

Look at this text and note the difference between the paraphrase and the summary that follows it.

> According to an AARP [American Association of Retired Persons] study, men and women over the age of 50 make up 25% of the total American workforce, but 40% of the self-employed. Now a new study reports that there is a growing trend among 3rd Agers toward entrepreneurship. According to the study, "The Coming Entrepreneurship Boom," the highest rate of entrepreneurial activity over the last decade belongs to those aged between 55 and 64. Surprisingly, the lowest rate belongs the 20-34 age group. Baby boomers are not over the hill just yet.

Paraphrase:

> Recent research shows that Americans aged 50 and over represent a quarter of those working. However, they represent 40% of those who work for themselves. A more recent investigation shows that more and more third agers are starting their own business. In fact, the report, "The Coming Entrepreneurship Boom" shows that the 55 to 64 age group is the most active in starting businesses. Younger individuals – aged 20 to 34 – are the least active in this area, showing that baby boomers are still an economic force.

Summary:

The latest research shows that Americans in the 55 to 64 age group are an economic force, representing a significant portion of those working or self-employed.

Notice how the paraphrased text uses different vocabulary and completely restructures the sentences. The only similarity between the original text and the paraphrase is the idea. The summary, on the other hand, has kept only the essential idea in much fewer words.

EVALUATING SOURCES

A key skill is being able to evaluate the credibility of a website or other source. You don't want to give readers false or inaccurate information. Here are some questions – based on work done at Stanford University – you should keep in the back of your mind whenever you evaluate a website.

- Does it look professional?
- Is it easy to check the truthfulness of the information?
- Is the content frequently updated?
- Is there a real organization behind the site?
- Does it clearly show professionalism in the content and services offered?
- Do the contributors show honesty and credibility?
- Is it easy to navigate and use?
- Are ads and offers kept to a minimum?
- Is the site error-free in form and content?
- Is it easy to contact someone?

Here are some popular and credible business sites. How would you rate these sites for credibility using the points mentioned above?

http://online.wsj.com/home-page

http://finance.yahoo.com/

http://www.money.cnn.com

http://www.businessweek.com/

http://www.fool.com/

ACTION CHECKLIST FOR STEP 5

	YES
1. I have access to a university or public library.	
2. I know how to take notes.	
3. I can use direct and indirect quotes correctly.	
4. I know the difference between summarizing and paraphrasing.	
5. I know how to judge the credibility of a website.	

STEP 6. Ask Questions

He who asks a question is a fool for five minutes;
he who does not ask a question remains a fool forever.
Chinese Proverb

There are times when you are preparing your business writing that simply asking questions provides more reliable and faster information than doing "research." Interviews are research after all, so do not be afraid to ask questions.

For example, Craig could have asked a coworker for his boss' daughter's name rather than stalking his Facebook profile. For more serious papers, such as a proposal to a major client, interviewing staff and other high ranking employees might be much better than reviewing annual reports or going to Google the company webpage.

I often use interviewing and surveying with subject matter experts or potential clients to gather information, data, and opinions.

INTERVIEWING TIPS

Interviewing is an essential skill you should build if you want to be an effective business writer. It is clear that we have to brainstorm and do research, but interviewing is clearly a supplement and extension of research.

Choosing the correct interview platform usually depends on whom you are seeking information from and what you want to use that information for. You have a variety of potential tools at your disposal: email, phone, Skype, or in person. For example, to get quick information, a phone call should suffice. But if you must record the interview for security, social, or business reasons, you may want to record a phone call or an in person interview.

In today's high-tech communication world, there are many formats to choose from. I've done interviews in a variety of ways.

By email: I really like this technique because it saves time for both me and the interviewee. It also gives me a document already in digital format.

Here is an example of an email you could use to send to potential interviewees.

To: _____
From: Frank Bonkowski

Subject: An interview, _____?

Hi _____, my name is Frank Bonkowski. My partner, Craig Gonzales, and I run a website called www.businessenglishhq.com, devoted to teaching business English. I read your article (or book), _____, and I was impressed by your knowledge and expertise on the subject of

_____.

I think our readers would love to learn more about you and your work. Would you be open to either an e-mail interview or a telephone interview with us?

* If you are open to an email interview, we can send you five to 10 questions by email and you can send them back at your convenience. Your answers can be brief and it shouldn't take up much of your time.

- If you prefer a ten to twelve minute telephone interview with us, based on the same questions, we can arrange to call you at a convenient time for you.

In return for this interview, we would be happy to let you promote your book, website, or other services you offer on our website.

Please let me know what you think. To give you an idea of how your interview might look, here's an example of an email interview we did with an expert on
_____.

I look forward to working with you and hope you'd like to participate.

Thanks for your time.

Frank Bonkowski

Face-to-face. When sitting down with someone, I can **adapt** the interview to the person's answers. I can either take notes because I write fast or record the interview with some recording equipment.

By Telephone. I've used this technique many times with people from around the world or who are too busy to meet. I sometimes use a recording service to record the interview in MP3 and **download** it to my computer. Be sure to have a list of questions close by so you don't forget to ask important questions.

By Skype. If the subject matter expert I'm interviewing uses this tool it is one of my favorites.

It combines all the advantages of face-to-face and telephone interviewing. I'm also able to record the conversation.

Here are some questions you could ask if you were interviewing a businessperson about her marketing approach. The questions are based on Brian Tracy's "7 P's of Marketing" – people, product, positioning, price, packaging, place, and promotion.

EXAMPLE OF INTERVIEW QUESTIONS

People (niche)	What kind of people are in your niche (your particular market)? How did you find this out?
Product (content)	Describe it. What's its purpose? Why do people need your particular product now? How is your product different from similar products on the market? Why should people buy it from you?
Positioning (current offers)	Where does your offer fit into your niche? What's your irresistible offer?
Price	How much do you charge for the product? How do you determine price?
Packaging	How are you packaging your product so it makes the most money? What's the cost?
Place (distribution)	Where did you get information about your niche, such as organizations, websites, or social media platforms? How are you reaching people?
Promotion	Have you tested out the product? What's your marketing and sales strategy and process?

SURVEYING TIPS

Another research tool I have used in consulting and teaching is the survey. It is an excellent way to get feedback from a large group of people. If you are developing a market research strategy for your company, if you are a freelance consultant, or if you are just trying to fix your HR process, a survey is the quickest way to get data to support your argument or investigate any outstanding issues. When you write a persuasive piece, you will want data to prove your point.

If you would like your company to change a policy, results from a poll or survey could very well be the deciding factor. And by conducting a survey, you will have put in the work that so few people are willing to put in. You will be the best writer on your team if you have data to back up what you are trying to say.

You can survey people in person, give them a paper-based version of the questionnaire, or use Internet tools such as Kwik Surveys or Survey Monkey.

Some advantages of these websites are that they provide many different question types. They also tabulate the survey results, which makes it easy to gather and organize data.

Here are some things to keep in mind when preparing a survey:

- Be clear about which group or groups you are targeting.
- Have an idea of how many people you intend to survey.
- Think carefully about the kinds of questions you would like to ask.
- Make your questionnaire just long enough to achieve your objectives.

ACTION CHECKLIST FOR STEP 6

	YES
1. I know who to reach to get the information I need.	
2. I know how to write an appropriate email message.	
3. I know which method is best to use to interview the person/s: - email - face-to-face - telephone - Skype	
4. I know what specific questions I would like to ask.	
5. I know which online tool I am going to use to survey a group of people: - Kwik Surveys or - Survey Monkey	

WRAP-UP

In this second pre-writing phase you learned how to come up with new content by using three useful tools: brainstorming, doing research, and asking questions.

In Step 4, Brainstorm Ideas, you became more familiar with the techniques of mind mapping and the 5Ws plus H for collecting information.

In Step 5, Research the Facts, you learned what libraries and the Internet can offer in the way of online resources. You are also familiar with the techniques of note-taking, citing information properly, paraphrasing, and summarizing. You also are more conscious that not all websites are created equal. You know how to verify the credibility of websites by asking yourself some key questions.

Finally, in Step 6, Ask Questions, you became acquainted with some interviewing and surveying techniques. You saw examples of the kinds of questions you could ask about marketing a product or service.

In the next writing phase, **Structure the Document**, we'll look at three techniques for writing an effective document which are often neglected by native speakers of English: outlining, writing a draft, and developing the message.

ACTIVITIES

ACTIVITY 1. WORD POWER

Match the word or expression from the article on the left with its correct meaning on the right.

Word or expression	Meaning	Choices
1. Components	_____	a. methodical
2. Jot down	_____	b. give the key points
3. Old-fashioned	_____	c. judge the value
4. Quota	_____	d. biased information
5. Systematic	_____	e. accuracy
6. Warning	_____	f. transfer a file
7. Issue	_____	g. restate in another form
8. Summarize	_____	h. person who responds
9. Evaluate	_____	i. adjust
10. Propaganda	_____	j. elements
11. Truth	_____	k. a kind of category
12. Data	_____	l. advice to take note
13. Download	_____	m. prescribed number or percentage
14. Interviewee	_____	n. actual information
15. Types	_____	o. write
16. Adapt	_____	p. item
17. Cite	_____	q. outdated
18. Paraphrase	_____	r. quote or mention

ACTIVITIES █

ACTIVITY 2. SENTENCE COMPLETION

Choose the best word from the Word Bank to complete each of the following sentences.

WORD BANK			
recommendations	Internet	questionnaire	brainstorming
mind map	truth	facts	5Ws

1. A good way to support your message is by using appropriate _____.

2. Kwik Survey is an excellent tool for building a _____.

3. Asking who did something or why is was done are part of the technique known as the

_____.

4. A short business report will usually conclude with _____.

5. Free association is an effective technique to use for _____.

6. The reputation of the author is one way to evaluate a website's

_____.

7. One of the best ways to find information today is on the _____.

8. A smart way to organize your ideas is by using a _____.

ANSWERS TO ACTIVITIES

ANSWERS · **ACTIVITY 1. WORD POWER**

Word or expression	Meaning	Choices
1. Components	j	a. methodical
2. Jot down	o	b. give the key points
3. Old-fashioned	q	c. judge the value
4. Quota	m	d. biased information
5. Systematic	a	e. accuracy
6. Warning	l	f. transfer a file
7. Issue	p	g. restate in another form
8. Summarize	b	h. person who responds
9. Evaluate	c	i. adjust
10. Propeganda	d	j. elements
11. Truth	e	k. a kind of category
12. Data	n	l. advice to take note
13. Download	f	m. prescribed number or percentage
14. Interviewee	h	n. actual information
15. Types	k	o. write
16. Adapt	i	p. item
17. Cite	r	q. outdated
18. Paraphrase	g	r. quote or mention

ANSWERS TO ACTIVITIES

ANSWERS · **ACTIVITY 2. SENTENCE COMPLETION**.

1. A good way to support your message is by using appropriate facts.

2. Kwik Survey is an excellent tool for building a questionnaire.

3. Asking who did something or why it was done are part of the technique known as the 5Ws.

4. A short business report will usually conclude with recommendations.

5. Free association is an effective technique to use for brainstorming.

6. The reputation of the author is one way to evaluate a website's truth.

7. One of the best ways to find information today is on the Internet.

8. A smart way to organize your ideas is by using a mind map.

3. STRUCTURE THE DOCUMENT

Organizing or structuring your business document is a very important component of the writing process. In this section, we look at the foundation of your writing from **outlining** to writing a **draft** to developing the **message**.

WHY DO WE STRUCTURE?

Structuring your document (be it an email, memo, report, or analysis) is essential before you can start writing. You have already figured out who you are writing to, why you are writing, and what information you want to include. Structure takes the information you have gathered and puts it down in a way that most effectively achieves your goal. It's not enough to write; you have to inform or persuade, and the structure is just as important as the content when you inform or persuade.

Structure can help you:

* Understand and focus your message;

* Decide whether you need more material to support your main points;

* Choose an overall pattern for the document, such as using chronological sequence in describing a procedure;

* Link specific points to the overall pattern;

* Fill in missing points and eliminate unnecessary information;

* Arrange an effective order of major and minor points;

* Keep you on track; and

* Save time in the writing process.

STEP 7. Make an Outline

Plans are nothing; planning is everything.
Dwight D. Eisenhower

You know your audience, you've brainstormed the subject, and you've done your research. You are **bubbling** with ideas and information to impress and persuade your audience.

You're now ready to create an outline that will serve as the structure of your content. Think of your outline like the bones in your body. The research is your muscles, the persuasion is your organs, and your post-writing editing is your beautiful skin. Without your bones, your beautiful body would crumble to the floor. So too would a written document fail to achieve its goal if the outline – the skeletal structure – is not clearly defined with the end result in mind.

WHY WRITE AN OUTLINE

Many people do not see the point in creating outlines. And for emails or very short reports, it may be a short outline with multiple sections. But creating an outline does not necessarily mean the same thing for every document. An outline is a skeletal structure.

Whenever I write an email, I know what my purpose is and how I am going to structure my email to communicate and support my purpose. For example, if I need to critique someone's performance, I will use the "sandwich" method of critique, wherein I use the following structure [*Say something good – Criticize – Say something good*].

Now, before writing my email, I do not take out a note pad and write those three things; I know them in my mind. There is an outline, even if I do not physically write it down.

That is why many people don't think an outline is useful – they don't realize they are using outlines all the time. Yet, if you are a new English writer, or if every email or document you write is incredibly important for your professional success, you absolutely must take the time to create a good outline.

FIVE-STEP STRUCTURE FOR A SHORT REPORT

All documents have a different format and you will need to adjust your outline to reflect that. For example, a business research report has a standard format to which you can add your outline of main and minor points.

1. Provide a short introduction stating the purpose of the report.

2. Explain the procedure you followed.

3. Present the findings.

4. Draw some conclusions.

5. Make a few recommendations.

When you just sit down and write from the top of your head, ideas can get muddled. If you have an outline, you will know what you have to write and when you have to write it in order to get the desired outcome. An outline helps you organize your ideas in a logical and orderly way. It gives a detailed overview of what you are writing about. And it allows you to prove to your readers that your ideas are related.

As I mentioned before, an outline is usually divided into major and minor points. You can create an outline using either phrases or sentences. Some experts recommend the "sentence" format because it is clearer. It also helps you, the writer, clarify your thinking. It **enables** you to build a solid structure for your ideas.

AN EXAMPLE OF AN OUTLINE

Here is an example of the beginning of an outline for both formats. (Adapted from ***The Vest-Pocket Writer's Guide)***

Subject: Planning for an older population

Research shows that the proportion of older people to younger people in North American society is increasing. This demographic **shift** will require new planning for the future.

Outline 1: Phrases	Outline 2: Sentences
I. Evidence of the shift	I. Evidence of the shift in the ratio of older people is clear in the latest statistics.
A. The declining birthrate	A. The birth rate is declining. The average woman is having fewer children.
B. The changing death rate	B. The death rate is decreasing. Older people are living longer.
C. Population profiles for the future	C. The latest data give us a profile of future population ratios. Statistics indicate an older population.
1. Profiles based on current rates	1. We can predict the profiles if we assume the same birthrate and a lower death rate.

Remember that an outline is not a static tool. I find myself often revising an outline **on the fly** during the writing phase. I may see a new relationship among ideas or a new way to present information.

When you first start writing an outline, you have to treat it like your mind map, except that you are not trying to brainstorm ideas – the ideas are already there. Instead, you need to focus on getting the structure of your document organized so you can write in a coherent way.

Once you have an outline, you can start **writing a draft.**

ACTION CHECKLIST FOR STEP 7

	Yes
1. If I am writing an email, I know my purpose.	
2. If I am writing a short report, I know the 5-step structure to follow.	
3. I know the end result I want to achieve for the document I am writing.	
4. I know how to use the "sandwich" method of critique.	
5. In writing an outline, I know how to use a "phrase" format and a "sentence" format.	

STEP 8. Write a Draft

It is better to write a bad first draft than to write no first draft at all.
Will Shetterly

Now that the background work is done, it's time to start the writing process. Even though there are only 15 steps to writing an excellent business document, you don't actually start writing until Step 8. You have already done the bulk of the real work. You have figured out what you are going to say to get your desired outcome, and you have organized those thoughts in a logical way so as to most effectively get to your desired result. You have not actually started writing yet.

Even though you are prepared, you may find it hard to just start writing. Once you can get past that initial problem you'll start to move quickly and you will find the writing process easy.

The first draft is your brain dump of information. You have already outlined all of your key points, so as long as you keep your draft focused on the narrow topic you have set, you can write pretty much anything you want.

Do not try to make your first attempt perfect. Good writing – business or otherwise – requires several re-writes. There are no ifs, ands, or buts about it. You will edit, write, and rewrite many times. So, in Step 8 you simply put pen to pad, fingers to keys, and write your message.

16 TIPS TO WRITE A DRAFT

Here are some valuable tips and strategies for writing a draft:

- Set yourself a time limit for writing periods. Segments of two or three hours **interspersed** with frequent pauses work best.

- Create a **skeletal** document in Google Drive or Open Office based on the outline. A nice feature of Google Drive is that it allows you to see a revision history of your document.

- Use the outline feature of MS Word for longer documents. It's a fantastic tool for creating headings and subheadings and jumping around a document.

- Don't start at the beginning of a document. That usually comes later, perhaps in the second draft.

- Copy some of your research notes and thoughts into the related sections of the outline.

- Get your ideas down as quickly as possible. If you are not pleased with a word or the phrasing of sentence, you can return to the idea in Step 13, Revising.

- Aim to develop one idea per paragraph. Paragraphs usually begin with a topic or key sentence. Repeat key words or phrases to link your ideas even more forcefully.

- Try to write three to five sentences per paragraph. The shorter the paragraphs the better, especially for e-documents that will be read on the computer or tablet.

- Use linking expressions to connect sentences and paragraphs together smoothly, such as "however" to show contrast and "moreover" to add information.

- Include some pertinent details and examples to support your ideas. You can add more in Step 9, Develop the Message.

- Emphasize important points by putting them at either the beginning or end of the document.

- Write notes to yourself in **brackets** in the document to keep in mind what you need to develop.

- If you get stuck on a section, leave it and return to it later.

- Try to keep your writing as simple as possible. Avoid having too many "complex" sentences that may either confuse or bore the reader.

- Put spice and variety in your sentences by mixing short, direct sentences with longer ones, as a great chef would do for his best recipe (more about sentence variety in Step 14, Edit the Language).

- For really important documents for which you have done two or three drafts, ask for comments or feedback from a trusted colleague.

Creating a draft allows you to clearly put your information and research down on paper. It guides you right from the start in keeping your message unified, coherent, emphatic, and logical. It sets you up for the remaining steps, which include developing your message and fine-tuning your writing to be professional.

Do not worry about being 100% correct in your first draft – instead focus on getting all of the information out of your brain and onto paper.

ACTION CHECKLIST FOR STEP 8

	Yes
1. I know exactly what I want to say.	
2. I have in mind a logical order to my ideas.	
3. I have fixed a time limit for my writing session.	
4. I have broken down my document into coherent chunks with related ideas.	
5. I have gotten comments on my draft.	

STEP 9. Develop the Message

To be persuasive we must be believable; to be believable we must be creditable;
to be credible we must be truthful.
Edward R. Murrow

Do you wish to improve or change your situation? Do you want to move your business forward? Do you want to be effective internally in your business when presenting proposals, estimates, budgets, and reports? Do you want to succeed externally in your business when meeting new clients, closing a deal, selling your product, and obtaining new contracts?

As you already know, you need to be **creditable** and truthful when you write. You also need to be good - exceptionally good - at persuading and informing your boss, colleagues, clients, and potential clients.

SIX PRINCIPLES FOR INFLUENCING OTHERS

In his classic book, *Influence: The Psychology of Persuasion*, Dr. Robert D. Cialdini explains six psychological principles for influencing others.

1. Be generous in your dealings with others; show genuine concern and they will usually return the favour.

2. If you can get someone to commit to a course of action, they will usually respect the commitment.

3. People tend to do what others are doing.

4. If you are an authority figure, people will tend to follow your suggestions.

5.   People are easily persuaded by those they like.

6.   If people think something is scarce or in limited supply, they will tend to want it.

FIVE-STEP PATTERN FOR PERSUASIVE WRITING

How can you be more persuasive in your writing?

In business writing you are often faced with solving a problem situation. In turn, you are often tasked with presenting a solution and you will have to use your writing to convince colleagues that your solution is best. This, for example, is a typical pattern in persuasive writing.

1.   Describe the context of the problem: readers may need to know the history of the problem.

2.   Define the scope of the problem objectively: tell readers why the current situation needs improvement.

3.   Explain the solution: show readers how to solve the problem. Stress how practical and reasonable the solution can be.

4.   Visualize what's next: move your readers from the present situation to the new situation.

5.   Move to action: conclude by recommending your readers take a course of action.

SUGGESTIONS FOR PERSUASIVE WRITING

Here are some more suggestions for making your writing more persuasive.

·   Include specific examples, statistics, dates, percentages, or quotations to support your arguments.

- Avoid any unnecessary or obvious information so as not to waste the reader's time.

- Divide your document into sections and subsections that are visually appealing and easy to follow.

How can you be more informative in your writing?

Using visuals in your business documents is a great way to support the text and communicate key ideas. It is also an effective way to condense information and be informative without boring your readers.

A good example of effective use of visuals is *Slide:ology: The Art and Science of Creating Great Presentations* by Nancy Duarte. It's a book designed to teach using PowerPoint effectively. The author practices what she preaches to state her case. She uses a variety of visuals, including charts, timelines, cartoons, paintings, photos, mind maps and graphs.

RECOMMENDATIONS FOR USING TABLE AND FIGURES

Here are some recommendations for using tables and figures the smart way:

- When using a table (text in columns) or figure (a visual representation of results), refer to it in the text.

- The meaning of a table or figure should speak for itself and be clear to the reader.

- Place a table or figure in an appropriate place next to the text.

- Visuals should not duplicate the text.

- Use figures such as graphs and charts to present statistical information. Examples include pie charts to show relationships among multiple values and bar charts for comparisons and trends.

- Other useful figures include diagrams, drawings, and maps.

To be more persuasive and informative in your communication, you need to show credibility and be recognized as the expert. Show people that you have the qualifications to inspire them or have faith in your judgment. Showcasing information in a concise, compelling way allows you to develop a relationship with your readers. It will lend you credibility and shows them you are a person of your word and they can trust you.

ACTION CHECKLIST FOR STEP 9

	Yes
1. I am aware of the six psychological principles for influencing others.	
2. I can apply the six principles to different business situations.	
3. I can use the five-step pattern for solving problems in my business writing.	
4. I know how to use visuals effectively to be informative.	
5. I continue to learn how to be more persuasive and informative.	

WRAP-UP

So in this third writing phase, you learned why structuring your document is such an important step in delivering an effective message.

In Step 7, Make an Outline, you saw two ways of creating an outline: using either phrases or sentences. You learned about a five-step pattern for writing a persuasive text when dealing with a problem situation.

In Step 8, Write a Draft, you looked at a variety of tips and strategies to overcome writer's block and write a rough draft.

Finally, in Step 9, Develop the Message, you learned six valuable ideas for influencing your readers. You also found out about some simple strategies for making your writing more informative by using visuals effectively.

In the next writing phase, **Use Appropriate Writing Style**, we'll look at three techniques for writing an effective document that are often neglected by native speakers of English: outlining, writing a draft, and developing the message.

ACTIVITIES

ACTIVITY 1. WORDS IN CONTEXT

Words or expressions can have different meanings. Look up the following items in a dictionary. They are in **bold** in the text. Write down the meaning that the best fits the context.

Word or expression	Meaning
Bubbling	
Tip	
Format	
Enable	
Research	
Shift	
Rate	
On the fly	
Momentum	
Interspersed	
Skeletal	
Bracket	
Creditable	

ACTIVITY 2. READ TO UNDERSTAND

Mark each statement as T (true) or F (false) according to information in the text.

Statement	T / F
1. Writing an outline is an optional exercise for both formal and informal reports.	_____
2. It is important to stick to the point in presenting your message.	_____
3. Outlines that use "phrases" are preferred because they are easier to write.	_____
4. Good writers usually begin writing the business report with the introduction.	_____
5. In today's business world, short paragraphs are preferred over long paragraphs.	_____
6. A good way to make your document flow smoothly is by using connecting devices.	_____
7. Two kinds of tables include pie charts and bar graphs.	_____
8. An outline helps you distinguish between main ideas and secondary ideas.	_____

STRUCTURE THE DOCUMENT

ANSWERS TO ACTIVITIES

ANSWERS • ACTIVITY 1. WORDS IN CONTEXT

Word or expression	Meaning
Bubbling	Filled
Tip	A help hint
Format	Layout
Enable	Permit
Research	Systematic investigation
Shift	Change
Rate	Quantity or amount
On the fly	In a hurry
Momentum	Speed
Interspersed	Divided up
Skeletal	Partial
Bracket	Punctuation mark
Creditable	Reputable or respectable

ANSWERS TO ACTIVITIES ▇

ANSWERS · ACTIVITY 2. READ TO UNDERSTAND

Statement	T / F
1. Writing an outline is an optional exercise for both formal and informal reports.	F
2. It is important to stick to the point in presenting your message.	T
3. Outlines that use "phrases" are preferred because they are easier to write.	F
4. Good writers usually begin writing the business report with the introduction.	F
5. In today's business world, short paragraphs are preferred over long paragraphs.	T
6. A good way to make your document flow smoothly is by using connecting devices.	T
7. Two kinds of tables include pie charts and bar graphs.	F
8. An outline helps you distinguish between main ideas and secondary ideas.	T

■ 4. USE APPROPRIATE WRITING STYLE

Dale Carnegie, author of one of my favorite books, ***How to Win Friends and Influence People,*** said:

"There are four ways, and only four ways, in which we have contact with the world. We are evaluated and classified by these four contacts: what we do, how we look, what we say, and how we say it."

In today's knowledge economy, Carnegie's ideas relate to business writing as well. I understand that what I write and how I write it are critically important for my business success. You must understand the same thing.

Even though you have done research, outlined your writing, have a clear understanding of your audience, and know your objective, you absolutely must use correct writing style.

If you are a brilliant marketer trying to get a job on Madison Ave. in New York, you cannot simply have a good brain — you must also dress the part with nice suits and expensive shoes. Your writing can have the same effect.

Your writing might contain brilliant ideas. But if your writing style is incorrect, slow, ugly, and sloppy, your reader will immediately judge you and your content and fail to give you the attention your good ideas deserve.

The purpose of section 4 is to give you the tools and standard practices necessary to avoid making writing style mistakes in your business writing.

As a business professional, you want to put your best foot forward. This means paying attention to your writing style by:

- Being **clear** in your message

- Using an appropriate **voice** for your audience

- Employing exact **vocabulary** and sentence **variety**

Let's take a look at the three elements of good writing: **clarity**, **tone**, and **style**.

STEP 10: Practice Clear Writing

Hard writing makes easy reading.

An old adage

SIX RULES FOR GOOD WRITING

So what is the secret to communicating clearly and concisely in business writing? George Orwell, author of ***Animal Farm*** and ***1984***, knew a few things about writing effectively. He proposed six simple rules for good writing:

1. Never use a metaphor, simile, or other figure of speech that you are used to seeing in print.

2. Never use a long word where a short one will do.

3. If it is possible to cut a word out, always cut it out.

4. Never use the passive where you can use the active.

5. Never use a foreign phrase, a scientific word, or a jargon word if you can think of an everyday English equivalent.

6. Break any of these rules sooner than say anything outright barbarous.

These rules can be difficult even for native English speakers, but don't get discouraged. According to Kenneth Davis, author of ***Business Writing and Communication***, "writing is a process that can be managed like any other business process."

Let's dig deeper into Orwell's classic advice.

1. AVOID COMMON SIMILES AND METAPHORS

Many native English speakers do not know the meaning of a "figure of speech." Figures of speech are expressions used in a non-literal way to create a special effect. For example, when someone says they can "see the light at the end of the tunnel," they mean that while a problem or difficult situation may not be over, the person can see that they've nearly reached the end or conclusion.

A simile compares two things using "like" or "as." Example: "As hot as hell." A metaphor makes a comparison, but doesn't use "like" or "as." "Life is a roller coaster."

Beware: using common similes and metaphors too often makes for dull writing. And don't mix metaphors. As William Strunk and E. B. White say in *The Elements of Style*: "... don't start by calling something a swordfish and end by calling it an hourglass."

2. KEEP IT SIMPLE

Keep it simple by using plain English. Never speak over the head of your readers by showing off "ten-dollar" words.

Avoid	Use
advise	say / tell
cognizant of	know
commence	begin
facilitate	help
impact on	affect
per diem	per day
potentiality	potential
remunerate	pay
subsequent to	after
utilize	use

3. AVOID WORDINESS

Many native speakers of English make the mistake of using too many unnecessary words. Replace wordy expressions with one or two words when possible.

Avoid	Use
at this time	now
despite the fact that	although
do an analysis of	analyze
due to the fact that	because
he is a man who	he
in-depth study	study
in a situation in which	when
make a recommendation	recommend
it is necessary that	must, should
schedule a meeting	meet
this is a subject that	this subject
with the exception	except

4. USE THE ACTIVE VOICE

Many native English speakers also do not know the difference between the use of passive and active voices. Good writing requires the use of strong, precise verbs in the active voice. The subject acts on the verb. The passive voice, however, has its place.

Here is an example: The CEO **believes** that the company **should launch** a new marketing strategy.

In the passive voice, the action is emphasized rather than the actor: **It is believed** by the CEO that a new marketing strategy **should be launched**.

You can also use the passive to be diplomatic about not identifying the actor: The letter **was badly written**. The passive voice also creates an authoritative tone: Jim's document **should be read** by tomorrow.

5. ELIMINATE JARGON

You have to fit your language to the audience you are addressing. But you'll never go wrong by using Standard English to communicate your message.

The editors at *Business Writing Clear and Simple* recommend that you eliminate buzzwords, avoid technical language, and stay away from bureaucratic jargon.

Avoid	Use
brick and mortar business	physical business
core competency	competence / ability
downsize	dismiss or lay off
functionality	effectiveness / success
meaningful	actual / real
modality	method
paradigm	model
scope out	take an in-depth look
skill set	skills
streamline	simplify

ACTION CHECKLIST FOR STEP 10

	Yes
1. I am careful about my use of similes and metaphors.	
2. I use simple, plain vocabulary.	
3. I eliminate unnecessary words.	
4. I use the active voice as much as possible.	
5. I don't use business jargon.	

STEP 11. Project the Right Tone

We often refuse to accept an idea merely because the tone of voice
in which it has been expressed is unsympathetic to us.

Friedrich Nietzsche

Tone is a reflection of your attitude and personality. It also shows how you feel about the reader. Writing with the correct tone starts with keeping in mind your focus in writing: why you are writing, who you are writing to, what your readers know and expect, and how you want to achieve your purpose.

You should always create a warm, professional appearance. You also want to be confident and courteous, being respectful to your readers. Genuine respect and sincerity go a long way in winning the minds and hearts of readers.

SEVEN TIPS FOR BEING PROFESSIONAL

Here are some of the top tips for creating a courteous, warm, professional appearance in your writing.

- Be positive and respectful at all times, never negative or condescending. You want to avoid writing when you are angry or upset about something. You may say something you don't mean or insult the reader, only to regret it later.

- Don't aim to be "Mr. Nice Guy." You are not a yes-man in your company. Sometimes a more confrontation tone is necessary. Be honest with everyone in your writing.

USE APPROPRIATE WRITING STYLE

- Appear confident because you have researched (see Step 5, Research the Facts) and planned (see Step 7, Make an Outline) your writing. This makes your writing more forceful and persuasive. However, remember that it is better to be humble than overconfident. You want your audience to trust you, but you can let your writing speak for itself.

- Avoid sexist or discriminatory language. For example, when writing a business letter, you should use "To whom it may concern," or "Dear Sir / Madam," when you don't know the reader's gender. Other words to use: "executive" instead of businessman, "chairperson" instead of chairman, "humankind" instead of mankind, "salesperson" instead of salesman, and "spokesperson" instead of spokesman.

- Use contractions - I'll, We'd - when appropriate. It makes the writing sound warmer and conversational.

- When you have something negative to say, avoid using disagreeable language. Don't stress what was done poorly but rather what can be done better.

- Reread your documents several times to see if you have gotten the content right. This is part of the self-editing process (see Step 13, Revise the Contents.)

The tone of your writing is how your writing sounds in the "mind's ear" of your reader. You want your reader to respect you, but not fear you. You want your reader to like you, but not think you are best friends. You want your reader to either learn something from you or be persuaded to your way of thinking. In short, you want to be the man or woman people trust, respect, and learn from. You do that by (1) knowing your stuff, (2) writing well, and (3) having a written voice that sounds natural, warm, friendly, and smart.

ACTION CHECKLIST FOR STEP 11

	Yes
1. I am respectful and sincere in my writing.	
2. I'm always positive and never negative.	
3. I'm direct but polite when I need to be.	
4. I am confident because I have planned well.	
5. I use non-sexist language.	

STEP 12. Develop Your Style

I didn't have time to write a short letter, so I wrote a long one instead.

Mark Twain

Remember that the purpose of business writing is to get your point across clearly and concisely, without wasting your reader's time. You want to get to the point quickly and not ramble on as Mark Twain warned.

Everything I have said previously about clarity, conciseness and tone gives your writing its distinctive voice or style.

SEVEN TIPS FOR A DISTINCTIVE STYLE

Here are a few tips to remember about style in business letter writing.

* Use clear language and short, simple sentences that don't confuse readers or waste their time. Keep your sentences under twenty-five words.

* Make your writing look good by using the proper layout.

* Use action words such as "We recommend / suggest that . . ." rather than abstract words like "We think," or "We suppose."

* Avoid qualifying words, such as "maybe,""probably," or "might," that weaken your message.

* Write from the point of view of your company. Show your strengths and those of your company.

USE APPROPRIATE WRITING STYLE

- State your purpose in the first sentence.

- Keep your reader's needs and interests in mind.

- Never write above the level of your readers.

- Use lists to structure and simplify the presentation of information. Use parallel structure when writing lists (as I have done here) by beginning each point with the imperative: use, write, state, keep.

- Use quotations, anecdotes, or stories, when appropriate, to add some pizzazz or flair to your writing.

- End your letter with a "call to action," such as "When can we meet to discuss your questions about the project?"

As I mentioned at the start of this step, you want to want to get your point across quickly in anything you write; your readers are busy professionals.

In the article *How to Write for Busy Readers* found in his book *How to Write, Speak and Think More Effectively*, Rudolf Flesch came up with 10 simple tips for concise, forceful writing. I have already mentioned some of these tips in previous steps, but they are worth repeating.

10 RECOMMENDATIONS FOR FORCEFUL WRITING

Put these 10 recommendations into practice and your readers will give you the attention you deserve.

1. *Use few articles, prepositions, and conjunctions.* For example, replace "the evidence we have" with "evidence we have." Replace "and" with a comma or semicolon.

2. *Use pronouns rather than repeating nouns.* Instead of writing "the Internal Revenue Service" several times, use "it" or "they."

3. *Learn to "factor" expressions.* Instead of writing "operating revenue and operating costs," write "operating revenue and costs."

4. *Use the active rather than the passive voice.* Instead of writing "Your assistance is needed," write "Please help us."

5. *Use verbs rather than nouns.* Instead of writing "We have information," write "We know."

6. *Use contractions.* Instead of writing "do not," write "don't."

7. *Use short names.* After you write "the Society for the Prevention of Cruelty to Animals," just write the Society.

8. *Use figures, symbols, abbreviations.* Using abbreviations for common entities or ideas makes writing flow much better. For example, most people will know what I.Q. means or what the IRS is.

9. *Use punctuation to save words* - Flesch's favorite space-saving device: the colon.

10. *Cut all needless words.* Instead of writing "factual information," write "facts."

At the end of his article on pages 291-292, Flesch leaves us with two messages. Which one is more concise and time saving?

> **Message 1:** "According to our agreement your company is to furnish services periodically on alternate days of the week in amounts to be specified at irregular intervals. Due to circumstances beyond our control, we herewith ask you to interrupt your services for one period only, Effective Monday, May 30 ... Please note that services are to be resumed as of Wednesday, June 1 ... in the same amount and manner as heretofore."

> **Message 2:** "Please skip Monday." [to the milkman]

CLEARLY MESSAGE 2 LEAVES MUCH LESS ROOM FOR CONFUSION, NOT TO MENTION SAVING A LOT OF TIME AND EFFORT!

ACTION CHECKLIST FOR STEP 12

	Yes
1. I use short, simple sentences.	
2. I address the needs of the reader.	
3. I write on behalf of my company and not myself.	
4. I include a call to action.	
5. I try to use as many of Flesch's time-saving tips as possible.	

WRAP-UP

In this phase of the writing process, you learned why it is important to use clear, simple language, write with a professional tone, and have your unique voice.

In Step 10, Practice Clear Writing, you were introduced to six simple rules for good writing that the master stylist, George Orwell, developed. You were introduced to the kinds of "fancy" words to avoid.

In Step 11, Project the Right Tone, you learned some strategies for creating a professional tone, which is so important to delivering an effective message.

Finally, in Step 12, Develop Your Style, you discovered some useful tips for writing a persuasive business letter. You also learned some time-saving strategies for writing concisely and effectively.

USE APPROPRIATE WRITING STYLE

![] ACTIVITIES

ACTIVITY 1. TRUE OR FALSE

Mark each statement as T (true) or F (false) according to information in the text.

Statement	T / F
1. The passive voice is effective in many situations.	_____
2. It's almost impossible to learn how to write well in a foreign language.	_____
3. Dale Carnegie said that the most important thing is being nice to people.	_____
4. When using parallel structure, you use the same grammatical structure.	_____
5. You can use contractions in business letter writing.	_____
6. Figures of speech add a lot of color to your business writing.	_____
7. Include a call to action in any letters you write.	_____
8. Use words like "probably" to qualify your ideas.	_____

ACTIVITIES ■

ACTIVITY 2. WRITING IT RIGHT

Complete the sentences with the most appropriate word from the word banks.

WORD BANK			
value	drafts	dissatisfaction	attitude
confidence	research	negative	embarrassing
tone	warm	communications	reason

Writing Strategies in Business

Key writing strategies in business help 1. _____. Knowing how to craft an important letter or document enhances an executive's or an employee's 2. _____ to the organization. Business writing requires careful 3. _____, thought and discipline. The writer may create several 4. _____ before a final version is ready. It is important not to rush business writing, because communications errors in business are potentially 5. _____ and costly if they result in lost opportunities, confusion among employees, or customer 6. _____.

Selecting the proper 7. _____ is critical in business writing. Purdue University reports that tone reflects the writer's 8. _____ and approach to the message and the reader. A tone that is harsh and hurried may detract from the message and convey an unintended theme. Business letters, memos and reports should reflect 9. _____, sincerity, and courtesy. Understanding the 10. _____ for the correspondence helps set the right tone. A 11. _____ and friendly tone is suitable for congratulating an employee on an accomplishment, but a reprimand requires a tone that is clear, direct, and authoritative. 12. _____ messages such as a reprimand should not attack the person, but instead focus on the actions causing the reprimand.

USE APPROPRIATE WRITING STYLE

ACTIVITIES

WORD BANK			
chairperson	plain	gender	official
implies	suitable	avoid	audience
	language	neutral	

Nondiscriminatory 13. _____ is best for business writing. A business document should avoid stereotypical terms or phrases that imply 14. _____. For example, it is improper to send a party invitation for "managers and their wives." That 15. _____ that only men are managers. Inviting "managers and their spouses" is nondiscriminatory. It is also preferable to use 16._____ job titles when possible, such as "chairperson" instead of "chairman" when the business writer does not know if the 17. _____ is a man or a woman.

Business writers should usually 18. _____ complex terms and phrases, unless they are writing for a specific 19. _____ familiar with the terms. A nurse writing another health care 20. _____ may use words and phrases not 21. _____ for a similar memo for the patient. Usually, it's best to keep general business writing 22. _____ and simple.

ANSWERS TO ACTIVITIES

ANSWERS • ACTIVITY 1. TRUE OR FALSE

Statement	T / F
1. The passive voice is effective in many situations.	T
2. It's almost impossible to learn how to write well in a foreign language.	F
3. Dale Carnegie said that the most important thing is being nice to people.	F
4. When using parallel structure, you use the same grammatical structure.	T
5. You can use contractions in business letter writing.	T
6. Figures of speech add a lot of color to your business writing.	F
7. Include a call to action in any letters you write.	T
8. Use words like "probably" to qualify your ideas.	F

ANSWERS TO ACTIVITIES

ANSWERS · ACTIVITY 2. WRITING IT RIGHT

1. communications
2. value
3. research
4. drafts
5. embarrassing
6. dissatisfaction
7. tone
8. attitude
9. confidence
10. reason
11. warm
12. negative
13. language
14. gender
15. implies
16. neutral
17. chairperson
18. avoid
19. audience
20. official
21. suitable
22. plain

5. KNOW HOW TO SELF-EDIT

Suppose you are the head of the human resources department at a large company. You receive a résumé which includes the following sentence:

Hi, I'm intrested to here more about your compangy right now.
I'm working today in a furniture busness as a drawer.

What would you do? You might laugh. You might wince. But I doubt you would hire the person. The writer obviously did not respect the final phase of the business writing process: **self-edit your writing**. It cost that person dearly; she obviously didn't get the job.

If you are a business professional, you don't want poorly thought out and grammatically inaccurate letters and documents to reflect negatively on you or your company. You want to eliminate any communication barriers between your intent in writing and the reader's perception.

Kenneth Davis, author of *Business Writing and Communication*, says that a good writer could spend on average 54 minutes writing a business letter. Twenty minutes (40%) would go for pre-writing or planning the letter, 10 minutes (20%) for writing it and another 20 minutes (40%) for rewriting the text. The other four minutes would be for breaks. So it's clear that planning and editing are the most important part of the process.

Let's now focus on the self-editing process, a key step in getting your message right and having the biggest impact on the reader. There are three phases in this process: revising, editing, and proofreading.

Much of what you read online mixes up these three stages. Revising, editing, and proofreading are distinct steps with different purposes in the self-editing process.

Nevertheless, in my experience, they do overlap.

Revising has to do first with looking at the big picture and second with improving each paragraph. Editing, on the other hand, helps you to sharpen up your choice of words and sentence variety. Proofreading fixes up the mechanics of the document: grammar, spelling, punctuation, and capitalization.

STEP 13. Revise the Contents

One day I will find the right words, and they will be simple.

Jack Kerouac

So you have completed the first draft of the business document. What do you do next?

You put aside the text for an hour or two or even until the next day. You go back to the text with fresh eyes and you read it aloud. Ask yourself whether the text clearly states the message and supports it with the right content. Then you look at paragraph unity, development, and coherence.

LOOK AT THE WHOLE DOCUMENT

Ask yourself if you:

• Engage the reader from the start with a startling statement or a quotation. For example, someone once said, "All lasting business is built on friendship."

• State your purpose clearly.

• Use the right tone.

• Give enough background information or historical context to the reader.

• Answer possible questions the reader may have.

• Provide enough details and examples.

• Include any useless information.

- **Bore** the reader.

- Ask the reader to take action or make a recommendation.

- Need to share the document with an outside **trusted** reader for honest **feedback**, especially if the document has high importance.

Once you've answered these questions, it's time to make changes to the first **draft** of the document. You can add to, delete, or modify parts of the text to improve it.

LOOK AT EACH PARAGRAPH

Ask yourself if paragraphs:

- Fit well together in the overall organization of the document;

- Follow some organizational **principle**, such as chronology, order of importance or problem to solution;

- Have sufficient unity or coherence that includes a good topic sentence expressing one main idea;

- Have sentences that are properly sequenced and flow well;

- Contain material that may be false, inappropriate, or unnecessarily repetitive;

- Show adequate development with appropriate supporting details;

- Flow smoothly with enough transitional expressions to guide the reader;

- Include overviews at strategic points to summarize topics; and

- Are not too long (three to five sentences - the shorter the better for online reading) and include lists or subheadings.

USEFUL TRANSITIONAL EXPRESSIONS

Here are some transitional expressions that tie your writing together and make it easier for readers to follow your message.

Transitional expressions	Examples
To draw emphasis	Indeed, in fact, of course
To give an example	As an illustration, in other words, in simpler terms
To add something	Furthermore, moreover, equally important
To compare	In the same way, likewise, similarly
To contrast	On the other hand, conversely, be that as it may
To show cause and effect	Therefore, as a result, it follows that

PRACTICE REVISING

Suppose you are applying for a job with a new company. You want to send a cover letter to accompany your resume. In the table below, there are notes in the left column that you have jotted down. In the right column, develop each of the four paragraphs by writing two or three sentences. Then check our suggested paragraphs at the end of the section and revise your own writing.

Notes for Cover letter	Paragraph development
Paragraph 1 • Reason why I am writing • Where and when I found information about the job	A.
Paragraph 2 • What I have accomplished in past jobs • Specific accomplishments	B.
Paragraph 3 • How I can help the new company • Specific skills I have	C.
Paragraph 4 • Call to action • Closing comment	D.

*See suggested answers on next page.

If you are looking for one good reference guide, I highly recommend you get a copy of *The AMA Handbook of Business Writing* - a well-written and attractively presented resource. It contains three sections that present:

• Detailed comments on the writing process, ranging from "audience analysis" to "promotional writing;"

• A complete reference guide to grammar and business vocabulary; and

• A storehouse of business documents, including Abstracts, Brochures, Mission Statements, Reports, and White Papers.

ACTION CHECKLIST FOR STEP 13

	Yes
1. I engage the reader immediately with a compelling introduction.	
2. I state my purpose clearly and respond to reader needs and questions.	
3. My document makes a recommendation or invites the reader to take action.	
4. I use a main idea in each paragraph of the document, supported by specific details.	
5. I compose sentences that flow effectively because of signposts, transitional expressions, or repeated words.	

ANSWERS • PRACTICE REVISING

A - I am writing in response to the position of [job title] appearing in [ad source] on [ad date].

B - As I have stated in my enclosed résumé, I have a proven record of success in different management positions for one of the biggest manufacturers of health care products: [ABC company.] Furthermore, I enjoyed working in different positions within the company from product development to marketing and regulatory affairs. Indeed, this past experience qualifies me for the position you have advertised.

C - I am confident that I can:

- effectively undertake business development responsibilities;
- analyze markets, value new products, and develop growth strategies; and
- lead successfully project teams.

D - I would appreciate meeting you for an interview to illustrate how my qualifications and experience might match your needs. I look forward to speaking with you soon.

STEP 14. Edit the Language

I'm not a very good writer, but I'm an excellent rewriter.

James Michener

You are now satisfied with the overall text organization and paragraph development. It's time to pay attention to your choice of words and sentence variety.

As a non-NE speaker, choosing the right words and using a variety of sentences to make your writing interesting is a difficult challenge. You have to continually work at developing these skills.

GOOD WORD CHOICE

Here are some pointers on using the right word when writing.

- Know the difference between a word's *denotation* or literal meaning and its *connotation* or figurative meaning. For example, the word *mature* denotes someone who is an adult. On the other hand, the word may be associated with old age. Be careful how you use the word in your correspondence; it may insult someone.

- Know how to use a dictionary and thesaurus. Consult a dictionary when you are not sure of the literal meaning of a word or its denotation. Use a thesaurus to choose among words with similar meanings but which might have different connotations.

  For example, you could say that Bill Gates is a *shrewd* business person – meaning he's highly intelligent. You don't want to refer to him as a *scheming* person – meaning he is devious or dishonest. Check the dictionary for the meaning of synonyms.

KNOW HOW TO SELF-EDIT

◼

- Know how to choose synonyms carefully. Many synonyms may have similar meanings but very different connotations. For example, one of the most *famous* or favorably well known American presidents is Barack Obama. On the other hand, Richard Nixon is *notorious* or unfavorably well known for the Watergate Scandal.

Here are three sets of words that have similar denotations, but are not entirely synonymous:

- *Anticipate*: foresee something with pleasure / *Expect*: consider something likely to happen

- *Fewer*: a smaller number (There are usually *fewer* grammatical mistakes in the second draft.) / *Less*: a smaller quantity (Mid-level managers make *less* money than vice presidents of a company.)

- *Plan*: a program to accomplish an objective / *Scheme*: a systematic plan connoting a secret plot.

Whether we use formal or informal language depends on the context and to whom we are speaking. When we speak, we mostly use colloquial or informal language. Be careful about using colloquialisms in formal writing. Within a business context, we use more formal language when our audience consists of unknown readers.

On other hand, when we know the audience we can be less formal. For example, in one of the exercises in this book, I ask you to "figure out" the meaning of many words we referred to in the text. I used the more informal "figure out" than the more formal "solve" because I feel we have a close relationship. A dictionary will help you determine whether a word is formal or informal.

GOOD SENTENCE VARIETY

There are several writing tricks to keep readers interested in your writing. First, use different sentence patterns. We'll look at three kinds of sentence patterns with variations. Second, vary the length of your sentences. For example, you can alternate long and short sentence. Third, play with different ways to open sentences.

SENTENCE PATTERNS

· **Simple sentence** (using one independent clause):

e.g., Steve Jobs was a successful American entrepreneur.

· **Compound sentence:**

a) combining two independent clauses with a coordinating conjunction – think of "fanboys" - f—for, a—and, n—nor, b—but, o—or, y=yet, s=so;

e.g., Steve Jobs was a successful American entrepreneur, and he was co-founder of Apple.

b) combining two independent clauses with a semi-colon:

e.g., Steve Jobs was a successful American entrepreneur; he was co-founder and chairperson of Apple.

c) combining two independent clauses with a conjunctive adverb, such as however, therefore, hence, thus, moreover, and consequently:

e.g., Steve Jobs was a successful American entrepreneur; moreover, he helped develop the iMac, iPod, iPhone, and iPad.

KNOW HOW TO SELF-EDIT

- **Complex sentence:**

  a) combining a dependent clause with an independent clause using subordinating conjunctions, such as when, because, since, after, before, while:

  e.g., Steve Jobs was a successful American entrepreneur because he was a visionary thinker.

  b) combining a dependent clause with an independent clause using a subordinating conjunction, such as when, because, since, after, before, while at the beginning of the sentence:

  e.g., Because Steve Jobs was a successful American entrepreneur, he became very rich and famous.

- **Independent clause:**

  a) embedding a non-essential clause or phrase:

  e.g., Steve Jobs, a persuasive and charismatic business leader, helped develop the iMac, iPod, iPhone, and iPad.

  b) embedding an essential clause or phrase, which is necessary to the meaning of the sentence:

  e.g., Steve Jobs who was diagnosed with pancreas cancer in 2003 died eight years later.

SENTENCE LENGTH

Learn and practice the different sentence patterns and use them in your business writing. They'll give your writing variety and pacing and make your text more interesting.

Look at the example below and then compare it with the revised version. Notice how we've used different sentence patterns.

Example:

Steve Jobs was born on February 24, 1955 and died on October 5, 2011. He was an American entrepreneur and inventor. He was best known as the co-founder, chairman, and CEO of Apple Inc. Through Apple, he was widely recognized as a charismatic pioneer of the personal computer revolution. He was also recognized for his influential career in the computer and consumer electronics fields. He transformed "one industry after another, from computers and smartphones to music and movies..." Jobs also co-founded and served as chief executive of Pixar Animation Studios. He became a member of the board of directors of The Walt Disney Company in 2006. Disney acquired Pixar at that time. (adapted from Wikipedia, http://en.wikipedia.org/wiki/Steve_Jobs).

Revised:

Born on February 24, 1955, Steve **Jobs** died on October 5, 2011. He was an American entrepreneur and inventor, best known as the co-founder, chairman, and CEO of Apple Inc. Through Apple, he was widely recognized as a charismatic pioneer of the personal computer revolution and for his influential career in the computer and consumer electronics fields, transforming "one industry after another, from computers and smartphones to music and movies..." Jobs also co-founded and served as chief executive of Pixar Animation Studios; he became a member of the board of directors of The Walt Disney Company in 2006, when Disney acquired Pixar.

SENTENCE OPENINGS

Another way to add variety and spice to your writing is by starting sentences in different ways. See the example below and note how we created new sentences, putting emphasis on different parts of the sentence.

Example: Jobs took a job as a technician at Atari in 1974 after dropping out of Reed College in 1972 and later that year travelled to India in search of spiritual enlightenment.

Different ways to start a sentence:

- After dropping out of Reed College in 1972, Jobs took a job as a technician at Atari in 1974 and later that year travelled to India in search of spiritual enlightenment.

- In 1972, Jobs dropped out of Reed College; two years later he was working as a technician at Atari and travelling in India in search of spiritual enlightenment.

- While working as a technician at Atari, Jobs searched for spiritual enlightenment in India after dropping out of Reed College in 1972.

- Steve Jobs, after dropping out of Reed College in 1972 and getting a job as technician at Atari in 1974, travelled to India in search of spiritual enlightenment.

- Early in his life, Steve Jobs dropped out of Reed College in 1972, worked for Atari as a technician, and travelled to India to find spiritual enlightenment.

ACTION CHECKLIST FOR STEP 14

	Yes
1. I know the difference between the denotation and the connotation of key words in my document.	
2. I use a dictionary and thesaurus when I write.	
3. I am careful about using synonyms correctly.	
4. I practice different sentence patterns in the documents I write.	
5. I vary the way I open sentences.	

STEP 15. Proofread for Perfection

A synonym is a word you use when you can't spell the other one.
Baltasar Gracián, translated from Spanish

For both native and non-NE speakers, it is difficult to check for mechanical errors in grammar, spelling, punctuation, and capitalization. You can begin with spelling and grammar checkers to help you initially. But they won't necessarily do a **thorough** job.

This is such a technical topic it is best to get a good reference such as *The AMA Handbook of Business Writing*. Use a dictionary to check spelling - we're using American spelling for BEHQ. I like to use <u>TheFreeDictionary.com</u>.

PROOFREADING CHECKLIST

Learn more about the following points on your own. Check for:

1. Confusing words, such as affect (vb. to influence) vs. effect (n. a result) or Its (pronoun, belonging to) vs. it's (a contraction, it is).

2. Sentence errors

    a) agreement between subjects and verbs,

    b) incomplete sentences (not a complete thought),

    c) run-ons (go on too long without proper punctuation)

d) parallel construction (using similar grammatical structures - for example, nouns to start a list)

e) redundancy ("the manager, he...")

f) incorrect modifiers ("Arriving late, the desk was empty.")

Refer frequently to the Business English HQ blog for posts on common writing mistakes (http://www.businessenglishhq.com/article-archive/).

3. Punctuation does make a difference: "Eats shoots and leaves" is very different in meaning from "Eats, shoots and leaves." Type the expression into Google to find out why.

Know when to use the comma [,], semi-colon [;], colon [:], hyphen [-], dash [--], parenthesis [( )], brackets [ ], apostrophe ['], quotation marks [" .."], ellipsis marks [. . .], exclamation point [!] and italics.

4. Capitalization. The English language has simple rules for capitalization:

a) the initial word of a sentence or direct quotation and the pronoun "I;"

b) names of people, places and things;

c) certain abbreviations and titles, for example, Frank Bonkowksi, Ph.D.;

d) languages, religions, nationalities;

e) historical periods, days, months and holidays; and

f) words in the title of a book, film, and work of art, but not the articles, prepositions, or conjunctions, e.g., *The Elements of Style*

KNOW HOW TO SELF-EDIT

5. Commonly Misspelled English Words

absence	definition	knowledge	profession
accidentally	describe	laboratory	professor
accommodate	description	laid	prominent
accumulate	desperate	led	pronunciation
achievement	dictionary	lightning	pursue
acquaintance	dining	loneliness	quantity
acquire	disappearance	lose	quizzes
acquitted	disappoint	losing	recede
advice	disastrous	maintenance	receive
advise	discipline	maneuver	receiving
amateur	dissatisfied	manufacture	recommend
among	dormitory	marriage	reference
analysis	effect	mathematics	referring
analyze	eighth	maybe	repetition
annual	eligible	mere	restaurant
apartment	eliminate	miniature	rhyme
apparatus	embarrass	mischievous	rhythm
apparent	eminent	mysterious	ridiculous
appearance	encouragement	necessary	sacrifice
arctic	encouraging	Negroes	sacrilegious
arguing	environment	ninety	salary
argument	equipped	noticeable	schedule
arithmetic	especially	occasionally	seize
ascend	exaggerate	occurred	sense
athletic	excellence	occurrence	separate

attendance	exhilarate	omitted	separation
balance	existence	opinion	sergeant
battalion	existent	opportunity	severely
beginning	experience	optimistic	shining
belief	explanation	paid	similar
believe	familiar	parallel	sincerely
beneficial	fascinate	paralysis	sophomore
benefited	February	paralyze	specifically
boundaries	fiery	particular	specimen
Britain	foreign	pastime	statue
business	formerly	performance	studying
calendar	forty	permissible	succeed
candidate	fourth	perseverance	succession
category	frantically	personal	surprise
cemetery	generally	personnel	technique
changeable	government	perspiration	temperamental
changing	grammar	physical	tendency
choose	grandeur	picnicking	tragedy
chose	grievous	possession	transferring
coming	height	possibility	tries
commission	heroes	possible	truly
committee	hindrance	practically	tyranny
comparative	hoping	precede	unanimous
compelled	humorous	precedence	undoubtedly
conceivable	hypocrisy	preference	unnecessary
conferred	hypocrite	preferred	until
conscience	immediately	prejudice	usually

conscientious	incidentally	preparation	village
conscious	incredible	prevalent	villain
control	independence	principal	weather
controversial	inevitable	principle	weird
controversy	intellectual	privilege	whether
criticize	intelligence	probably	woman
deferred	interesting	procedure	women
definitely	irresistible	proceed	writing

ACTION CHECKLIST FOR STEP 15

	Yes
1. I use a good reference for grammar.	
2. I use the www.BusinessEnglishHQ.com blog for pointers on improving my writing and grammar.	
3. I pay careful attention to punctuation when writing in English.	
4. I am aware of rules for capitalization in English.	
5. I am consistent in the English I use for spelling, whether it is American, British, or Canadian English.	

WRAP-UP

In this final phase of the writing process – self editing, you learned some of the secrets good writers use to produce a professional, error-free document all the time.

In **Step 13, Revise the Contents**, you learned how to rework the document as a whole and how to improve your paragraphs, using techniques such as transitional expressions.

In **Step 14, Edit the Language**, you learned some strategies for choosing the right word and for varying your sentence patterns.

In **Step 15, Proofread for Perfection**, you distinguished among simple, compound and complex sentences and learned some ways to vary the way you begin a sentence.

 ACTIVITIES

ACTIVITY 1. WORD POWER

Match the word or expression from the article on the left with its correct meaning on the right.

Word or expression	Meaning	Choices
1. Wince	_____	a. coincide or go together
2. Hire	_____	b. reliable
3. Break	_____	c. specialized language
4. Overlap	_____	d. response
5. Coherence	_____	e. overused expression
6. Bore	_____	f. the noun referred to
7. Trusted	_____	g. pause
8. Feedback	_____	h. complete
9. Draft	_____	i. lose interest
10. Principle	_____	j. make a face
11. Cliché	_____	k. connecting words
12. Antecedent	_____	l. employ
13. Thorough	_____	m. being connected
14. Jargon	_____	n. stage in the development of a text
15. Conjunctions	_____	o. a rule

ACTIVITY 2. FIND THE MISTAKES

Correct the grammatical and mechanical mistakes (verb tenses, spelling, punctuation, capitalization) in the following texts.

1. Facebook is now the biggest social network in world. It's the one with the most subcsribers. Facebook reach over 900 million users this year and was available in all the countres of the world. It is posible for every single person to be connected to Facebook because it is available in most language. It also allows translation into others languages, so everyone can comunicate on Facebook no matter where you leave or what language you speek. In adition, the site has million of games applications and uses. More and more people are used it daily in there lives.

2. While the history of internet begin in the middle of the 1950s, it becomes what we know about it around the mid 90s. Since than, it has a great impact on culture and the commerce, mainly by give us the largest communication service. Its includes electronic emailing, instant mesaging, social network, discussion forums and the blog. Internet is now a useful tool integrate into people daily lives. However Internet addiction becomes a real society problem, especially with the arrival of the latest socials networks.

3. In recent year, our society witness the rise of the Internet. Now, the web becomes part of his lifestyle. we communicate through the Internet we buy it and we learn throught it. In other word, we can do virtual anything on those platform. With this useful tool, one would think that it is the perfect combination of functuality and usefulness. But don't fool themselves. Like all things, the Internet has it good and bad sides Have we become addict to the Internet? The statistics speaks for themselves. We reached a point

▮ ACTIVITIES

of no return In 2006, 18% of the worldwide population use the Internet. 5 years later, the same survey show that 35% of the global population is connected to the Web. That be equal to a 200% rises in only five year.

ANSWERS TO ACTIVITIES ▪

ANSWERS • ACTIVITY 1. WORD POWER

Word or expression	Meaning	Choices
1. Wince	j	a. coincide or go together
2. Hire	l	b. reliable
3. Break	g	c. specialized language
4. Overlap	a	d. response
5. Coherence	m	e. overused expression
6. Bore	i	f. the noun referred to
7. Trusted	b	g. pause
8. Feedback	d	h. complete
9. Draft	n	i. lose interest
10. Principle	o	j. make a face
11. Cliché	e	k. connecting words
12. Antecedent	f	l. employ
13. Thorough	h	m. being connected
14. Jargon	c	n. stage in the development of a text
15. Conjunctions	k	o. a rule

ANSWERS TO ACTIVITIES

ANSWERS · ACTIVITY 2. FIND THE MISTAKES

1. Facebook is now the biggest social network in the world. It's the one with the most subscribers. Facebook reaches over 900 million users this year and is available in all the countries of the world. It is possible for every single person to be connected to Facebook because it is available in most languages. It also allows translation into other languages, so everyone can communicate on Facebook no matter where you live or what language you speak. In addition, the site has millions of games, applications, and uses. More and more people are using it daily in their lives.

2. While the history of the Internet began in the middle of the 1950s, it has become what we know about it around the mid-90s. Since then, it has had a great impact on culture and commerce, mainly by giving us the largest communication service. It includes electronic emailing, instant messaging, social networks, discussion forums and blogs. The Internet is now a useful tool integrated into people's daily lives. However, Internet addiction has become a real societal problem, especially with the arrival of the latest social networks.

3. In recent years, our society witnessed the rise of the Internet. Now, the web has become part of our lifestyle. We communicate through the Internet, we buy through it, and we learn through it. In other words, we can do virtually anything on this platform. With this useful tool, one would think that it was the perfect combination of functionality and usefulness. But don't fool yourself. Like all things, the Internet has its good and bad sides. Have we become addicted to the Internet? The statistics speak for themselves. We have reached a point of no return. In 2006, 18% of the worldwide population used the Internet. Five years later, the same survey showed that 35% of the global population was connected to the Web. That is equal to a 200% rise in only five years.

FINAL WORDS

■ FINAL WORDS

Congratulations! You have completed the Business English HQ 15-step system for communicating effectively in your business writing.

If you worked through all the steps and activities, you are now well equipped with a simple, systematic approach to writing. You have enriched your vocabulary, polished your sentence style, and improved your paragraph organization and development. In the process, you have also sharpened your reading skills.

Keep the book with you whenever you have to write a business document – a letter, an email, a proposal, a business plan, or a report. Refer to the storehouse of tips and strategies contained in the each of the 15 Steps.

Continue to improve your writing. By writing well, you'll look competent and professional and be admired by your colleagues or superiors. You'll gain that competitive edge that will bring your career to another level.

Wishing you business success!

ABOUT THE AUTHORS

FRANK BONKOWSKI

Frank Bonkowski is an educational writer, ELT teacher and trainer, business consultant, and web publisher.

As an educational writer of language learning materials, he's consulted on nine textbook projects, both as course writer and project manager in some cases. He designed, managed and co-authored a two-level series of adult-level ESL textbooks, entitled *Canadian Snapshot*s, published by Pearson Longman ESL.

He co-authored the five-level high-school English-second language *Take* series, published by ERPi of Montreal, which earned over $27 million in revenues. He participated in the writing of two other English-second language textbooks for publishers in Montreal and Toronto, Canada.

As a university teacher specializing in ELT, he has taught at McGill, Concordia, and TELUQ, a center of distance education. At McGill, he directed the teacher-training program at the Faculty of Education. At TELUQ, he created a series of four university-level distance education courses in ELT for teacher training. He has also taught at several colleges, including the Cegep Saint-Laurent.

As a business consultant, he was director of an ESL division of a publishing company. In addition, as representative of a firm specializing in mergers & acquisitions for small businesses, he was president of a chapter of Business Network International in Montreal for one year.

As a web publisher, he has written extensively about adult transition and reinvention at Happiness in Midlife (http://happinessinmidlife.com/). He co-authored and produced several e-books, e-courses, audio programs, and podcasts in collaboration with experts in midlife issues.

CRAIG GONZALES

Craig Gonzales has been helping students learn writing, reading, math, and business for the last 11 years. He has worked in the US, Mexico, Ghana, Singapore, and Thailand, and is currently co-founder of Business English HQ. His background is in business, finance, and liberal arts. He is in the process of developing a low-cost curriculum in test preparation.

■ USEFUL WEBSITES AND BUSINESS WRITING BOOKS

www.BusinessEnglishHQ.com

Owl, the Purdue Online Writing Lab (http://owl.english.purdue.edu/owl/section/4/16/)

Rutgers University Business Research Guide (http://libguides.rutgers.edu/business).

Business Writing Clear and Simple. New York: Learning Express, 2007.

Davis, Kenneth. *Business Writing and Communication*. New York: McGraw Hill, 2010.

Fitzpatrick, Dale, and Kathleen Vance. *Writing for Success: Preparing for Business, Technology, Trades and Career Programs*. Don Mills, Ontario: Prentice Hall Canada, 1998.

Flesch, Rudolf. *How to Write, Speak and Think More Effectively*. New York: Penguin Books, 1960.

Guffey, Mary Ellen, and Dana Loewy. *Business Communication: Process and Product*. Mason, OH: South-Western Cengage Learning, 2011.

Strunk, William, and E.B. White. *The Elements of Style*. New York: The Macmillan Company, 1959.

Wilson, Kevin, and Jennifer Wauson. *The AMA Handbook of Business Writing*. New York: American Management Association, 2010.

REVIEW REQUEST

Good reviews are important to the success of our book.

If you enjoyed this book or if you found it useful, Craig and I would be grateful if you'd post a positive review. Your support is important and it truly makes a difference. We read all reviews so we can benefit from your feedback.

If you'd like to leave a review, please go to the review section on the book's Amazon page (put hyperlink). You'll see a large button saying, "Write a customer review" – click that and you're ready to go!

Thanks again for your support.

Wishing you business success.

Frank and Craig

◼ PURCHASE *WRITE NOW* IN BULK

Could individuals at your company, organization, or educational institution write better? You bet they can by studying and using the strategies and tips in *Write Now*.

Write Now is a valuable resource and guide for giving you high-level business writing skills to gain a competitive edge.

Get significant price breaks for purchasing in bulk at 11+, 51+ and 501+ copies.

For more information, contact me directly at frank@businessenglishhq.com.

SPOT ANY ERRORS?

We have put into practice what we preach in this book on business writing. We have revised the contents, edited the language, and proofread the text many times, but there still may be errors and typos.

If you find anything that should be corrected or changed, please let me know. You can contact me directly at frank@businessenglishhq.com.

Want to make any comments?

I'd love to get your feedback about what we can improve as well as your ideas about what we can add to the next edition. You can contact me directly at frank@businessenglishhq.com.

INDEX